ENGLISH RE-START

RE*START

ENGLISH

BASIC

NEWRUN

40개국 이상에서 출판!
세계가 인정한 학습서가 왔다

성경 다음으로 가장 많이 팔린 이 책은 1945년 출간된 뒤 40개국 이상에서 출판된 베스트셀러이자, 가까운 일본에서도 30년 이상 사랑받고 있는 책입니다. 시간이 흘러 세상은 변해도 이 책의 가치는 여전히 빛나고 있습니다.

저자인 I.A 리처드(1983~1979)는 20세기 영어권 문예비평가로 언어 감각의 달인으로 평가받았습니다. 그는 1930년부터 8년 동안 중국에 머물며 영어와 영문학을 가르쳤고, 1940년대에는 미국 메사추세스 주에서 외국인에게 영어를 가르치기도 했습니다.

리처드는 이렇게 오랫동안 영어를 가르치면서 '모국어 간섭 없이 영어를 배우는 것이 좋다'는 생각을 하게 되었다고 합니다. 그 뒤 많은 실험과 연구를 통해 단계적 직접법(Graded Direct Method)이란 학습법을 만들게 되었고, 그 학습법을 기반으로 이 책은 탄생하였습니다.

일본에는 이 학습법이 1947년 동경여자대학 교수 콘스타스 차펠에 의해 소개되었고, 그 뒤 하버드 대학에서 리처드에게 직접 배운 요시자와 미에가 교사 양성 트레이닝을 시작하며 본격적으로 활성화되기도 했습니다. 일본에서는 지금까지도 'GDM 영어 교수법 연구회'에 의해 연구 활동이 이어지고 있을 만큼 훌륭한 학습법으로 자리 잡았습니다.

이렇듯 현장에서 50년 이상 폭넓은 조사와 테스트가 이어지면서 책의 내용이 학습법과 더욱 발전하였고, 이 책을 통해 몇 백만 명에 달하는 전 세계의 독자가 이미 영어를 배우는데 성공하였습니다.

세상에서 가장 쉽고 간단히 영어를 끝낼 수 있는 책으로 평가받는 이 책을 펼치는 순간 깜짝 놀라실 겁니다. 한글 해석은 하나도 없고 오로지 영어 문장과 그림만 있기 때문이죠. 그리고 자신도 모르게 영어와 그림을 보며 책장을 넘기는 자신을 발견하고는 한 번 더 놀라게 될 겁니다.

우리는 단어를 모르더라도 손짓과 발짓으로 많은 걸 표현할 수 있지요. 이 책에는 그런 손짓 발짓 영어가 아주 심플한 그림으로 표현되어 있습니다. 나를 가리키며 I라고 말하고, 상대방을 가리키며 You라고 말하는 것 그대로를 그림으로 표현해놓은 것이죠. 이렇게 그림으로 모든 걸 명쾌하게 표현했기 때문에 해석을 거치지 않아도 영어를 이해할 수 있는 거랍니다. 여러분은 그림과 문장을 반복해서 보기만 하면 됩니다.

영어 공부를 어떻게 시작할지 막막하다면 이 책은 아주 특별해보일 겁니다. 문법, 단어, 발음을 몰라도 말하기, 듣기, 읽기를 한 번에 해결할 수 있기 때문입니다. 게다가 혼자서도 충분히 끝낼 수 있으니 더욱 매력적이라고 할 수 있죠.

여러분은 어느 정도의 영어 실력을 갖추고 싶으세요? 이 책은 살면서 영어 때문에 불편하지 않을 만큼의 내용을 담았습니다. 딱 이만큼만 영어 하면 좋겠다는 사람들을 위한 이 책은 미국 중학생 수준의 영어를 할 수 있도록 도울 것입니다.

말하기·듣기·읽기를 한 번에 끝낸다!

말하기, 듣기, 읽기, 쓰기가 한 번에 된다 처음 말을 배울 때는 듣고 말하고 읽고 쓰는 학습을 유기적으로 반복하듯, 이 책 역시 그 원리가 구현되도록 했습니다. 그냥 반복해서 읽고, 따라 말해보고, MP3를 활용해 듣고 따라 써보면 자연스럽게 4가지 기능이 향상되는 것을 느낄 겁니다. 학습자의 수준과 환경에 따라 다르겠지만 대부분의 사람들은 한 달 정도면 몰라보게 실력이 달라지는 것을 느낄 수 있을 것입니다.

중학교 수준의 단어로 구성했다. English Re-start 시리즈(이하ER)는 가능한 적은 단어로 일상생활을 표현할 수 있게 했습니다. ER에는 300개의 단어가 ER Advanced 1권에는 ER에 나온 300단어와 새로운 단어 450개를 포함 750단어가 사용되었습니다. 그리고 이 750개의 단어는 ER Advanced 2권에서 1000개의 단어를 자유롭게 사용하기 위한 기초가 됩니다. 쉽고 중요한 단어부터 순서대로 반복하여 등장하기 때문에 무리하게 외우지 않아도 자연스럽게 기억됩니다. 이 단어들만 알아도 영어 커뮤니케이션은 전혀 문제없습니다.

단순한 그림으로 이해력을 높인다 이 책의 그림은 문장의 의미를 선명하게 보여주기 위해 최대한 단순하게 그렸습니다. 각 문장을 선으로 그린 그림으로 표현하여 학습자가 문장의 패턴이나 단어에 집중할 수 있도록 배려했습니다.

자연스럽게 반복학습이 가능하다 이 책은 한 페이지에서 배운 말이나 문장이 다음 페이지의 단어나 문장을 배우는 데 도움이 되도록 구성하였습니다. 앞에서 배운 내용을 뒤에서 반복하는 동시에 새로운 내용을 추가로 배우기 때문에 따로 복습하지 않아도 됩니다. 읽다 보면 자연스럽게 이해하고 기억하게 될 것입니다.

Question과 Workbook은 보너스 이 책은 본문과 Question, Workbook으로 나뉩니다. 본문은 그림과 영어문장만으로 이루어진 부분을 가리키며 대부분의 페이지를 차지합니다. 하지만 내가 확실히 알고 있는지 점검하기 위해 Question, Workbook 코너를 따로 두었습니다. 이 두 코너는 정답을 쓰면서 확인한 후 소리 내어 말해보면 더욱 효과가 큽니다.

이 책의 간단한 활용법 그림과 문장을 가볍게 끝까지 훑어보는 것이 중요합니다. 그림은 오른쪽 순서대로 보세요. 그 다음 소리 내어 읽어보세요. 외우려 하지 말고 몇 번만 반복해서 읽어보세요. 머릿속에 그림이 떠오르고, 입으로는 말을 하게 될 겁니다. Question과 Workbook 코너를 통해 자신의 실력을 확인해보는 것도 좋습니다. 무료로 제공되는 MP3를 들으면서 따라 말해보세요. 아울러 책에 나와 있는 그림을 크게 모션을 취하면서 따라 말해보면 더욱 좋습니다.

MP3는 cafe.naver.com/newrun 에서 다운로드 받을 수 있습니다.

하루만에 회화학원 3개월 다닌 느낌이 나요!

이 책을 한국에 소개하면서 〈ENGLISH RE-START 체험단〉이란 이름으로
독자 여러분을 초대하여 일주일 정도 공부하는 자리를 마련했습니다.
참여해주신 서현지(여/23살/대학생) 씨가 올려준 내용을 요약 소개합니다.

첫째 날! 회화 학원 3개월 다닌 효과가 느껴지던데요. 첫날은 지하철에서 책을 훑어보는 것부터 시작했어요. 옆에 사람이 신기한 듯 책을 계속 쳐다보더군요. 아주 간단한 그림과 문장을 연결시켜놓았는데 아무리 공부해도 감이 안 잡히던 other, another 등 이런 말들이 뭐랄까 감이 잡히더라고요. 왜 회화학원 다녀도 머리로는 아는데 입으로는 안 나오던 문장들 있잖아요. 그런 말들을 나도 모르게 중얼거리게 되더라고요. 무엇보다 회화에 자신감이 생겨 좋았습니다. 덧붙이면 저희 어머니께서 이 책을 보시더니 출판되면 꼭 하나 사달라고 하시더라고요. 재미있고 쉬워 보였나봅니다! 나중엔 엄마랑 같이 공부해야겠어요~

둘째, 셋째 날! 헷갈리는 단어가 그림으로 다 생각나요. 영어 문장은 복잡해졌는데도 그림은 계속 간결하네요! 오늘은 어제 배운 것들도 나와서 자연스럽게 복습하였고 새로운 단어, 문법, 문장도 배울 수 있었습니다. take off란 동사는 매번 생각이 잘 안 났는데 오늘 그림 한 컷으로 확실히 정리가 되었어요. 이렇게 헷갈리는 단어, 숙어들이 그림으로 기억되면서 책을 덮어도 다 생각나는 거예요. 전치사도 헷갈리지 않게 복습할 수 있어서 좋았습니다! 근데 이 그림, 볼수록 맘에 들어요~

넷째 날! **영어회화에 많이 쓰이는 단어가 보여요.** 오늘 공부한 부분은 회화에 도움이 많이 될 것 같네요. 앞에 나온 내용이 반복되면서 새로운 내용이 등장해 저절로 복습이 되더라구요. 특히 짧은 문장에서 서서히 긴 문장으로 확장되면서 단어들이 반복되니까 그 단어의 의미도 정확히 알게 되었고, 단어들의 시제 변화까지 볼 수 있었답니다. 이야기가 짧은 꽁트 같아서 책 보는 재미도 쏠쏠 했어요!

다섯째, 여섯째 날! **발음이 고쳐져요.** 오늘은 MP3파일을 들으면서 했는데요. 처음에는 MP3속도가 좀 느리단 생각이 들었어요. 그런데 들으면서 따라해보니 속도가 딱 적당하더라구요. 발음도 정확해서 발음 교정에도 좋을 것 같습니다. 집에서 들을 때는 실제로 그림처럼 행동을 해봤는데 처음에는 민망하다가 나중에는 재밌어졌어요. 그리고 나니 확실하게 기억되어 죽어도 안 까먹을 것 같더라구요.^^ 외우려고 하지 않아도 자연스럽게 외워지는 것 같아서 기분이 좋았답니다.

마지막 날! **문법, 단어, 듣기, 말하기 한 번에 되요** 책으로 공부하고, 지하철이나 버스 안에서 MP3를 듣고 중얼거리면서 복습하기에 딱 좋은 것 같아요. 내용이 어렵지 않아서 그런지 책 없이 MP3만 듣고도 그림이 떠오르는 장면이 꽤 있었어요! 나도 모르게 떠오르는 그림들을 생각하면서 정말 신기했답니다! 아무래도 이 책의 가장 큰 장점은 문법, 단어, 듣기, 말하기를 한 번에 연습할 수 있다는 거 같아요. 주변 사람들에게 완전 추천해주고 싶습니다. 특히 저희 부모님? 특별한 영어공부 해보게 돼서 너무 좋았어요!

영어 한 달만 다시 해봐야겠어요!

〈ENGLISH RE-START 체험단〉 활동에 참여해주신 분들이 남겨주신 글입니다.

온몸으로 하는 영어 공부, 적극 추천! 직접 모자와 테이블을 갖다 놓고 문장을 읽어보며 해봤는데, 훨씬 더 그림을 이해하기 쉬웠습니다. 와~ 정말 신기해요!

– 이춘호, 남, 31세, 회사원, kjj2949

put on, 더 이상 헷갈리지 않아요! 쉽지만 항상 헷갈렸던 put on 같은 숙어들이 워크북을 공부하면서 깔끔하게 정리 되었습니다. 여기에 나와 있는 표현들을 잘 익혀두면 토익에 큰 도움이 될 듯싶네요!

– 최광식, 남, 28세, 고시생, lumplant

시제 고민은 이제 그만! 제가 생각한 베스트 컷은 English Re-start 38~39 page의 그림이었어요. 한글 설명 없이도 이해가 되다니…. 다양한 행동과 연속적인 그림을 통해서 시제 변화와 개념을 확실히 알게 되었어요.

– 김경자, 여, 38세, 회사원, flqj1004

자연산 영어 그대로를 즐기는 방법! 그림으로 보는 게 해석된 문장을 보는 것보다 은근히 해석이 쉬워요. 그동안 영어를 배웠던 느낌과는 전혀 달라요. 진짜 영어가 흡수되는 느낌? 아주 좋아요!

– 김재희, 여, 33세, 컨설턴트, jesusbarag17

10년 묵은 '관사' 체증, 이제야 풀리네요! 영어 공부를 하다가 제일 헷갈리는 게 a, the 등 관사인데, 이 책만큼 쉽게 관사의 느낌을 이해하게 되는 책은 처음 봤어요. 그림과 문장만 봤을 뿐인데, 아아 관사가 이런 거구나 싶더라고요.

- 오재학, 남, 24세, 대학생, happyjjory

소리 내서 공부하니 발음도 잡히네요! 소리를 내면서 읽었는데, 상당한 효과가 있더군요. 쉬운 문장이긴 하지만 억양이라든가 발음에 있어서도 다시 한번 잡아준다는 느낌도 받았고요. 진작 이렇게 공부했으면 지금쯤 발음 걱정 없을 텐데 말이죠!

- 진우경, 남, 29세, 마케터, goorm1226

자투리 시간에 딱이에요! 지하철에서 작게 소리 내어 읽으면서 공부했는데, 자투리 시간을 활용해서 영어 공부도 하니 도착지까지 시간이 금세 가더군요! 새롭게 알게 된 표현들도 많았습니다.

- 유모란, 여, 25세, 취업준비생 rhaxodn

눈 딱 감고 한 달만 다시 해보려고요! 영어 공부를 한 지가 정말 오래되서 어디서부터 다시 시작해야 할지 막막했는데... 이 책을 보면서 영어를 이렇게 다시 시작할 수도 있겠다는 용기를 얻었네요! 눈 딱 감고 한 달만 해볼랍니다! 아자!

- 정영희, 여, 51세, 주부, jyh0212

CONTENTS

English Re-start Basic

English Re-start Basic

I

YOU

I

YOU

HE

SHE

IT

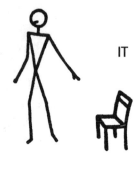

THEY

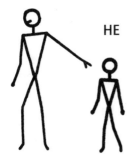 HE

 THEY

 IT

 THEY

I am here.

He is there.

She is here.

She is there.

It is here.

It is there.

They are here.

They are there.

You are there.

You are there.

You are here.

We are here.

It is there.

They are there.

We are here.

They are here.

This is a man.

This is a woman.

That is a man.

That is a woman.

This man is here.

That man is there.

This woman is here.

That woman is there.

This is a table.
This table is here.

That is a table.
That table is there.

It is there.

It is here.

This is a hat.
It is a hat.

This is a hand.

This is the thumb.

These are the fingers.

This is my head.

This is my hat.

My hat is in my hand.
It is in my hand.

My hat is on my head.
It is on my head.

This is
my hat.

That is
his hat.

His hat is
on his head.

Her hat is in
her hand.

That is your hat.
It is on the table.

Those are your hats.
They are on the table.

These are my hands.

Those are your hands.

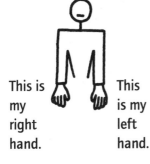

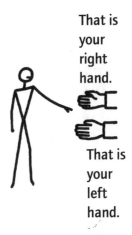

This is
my
right
hand.

This
is my
left
hand.

That is
your
right
hand.

That is
your
left
hand.

His hat is on the table.

He will take his hat off the table.

He is taking it off the table.

He took it off the table.

He will put his hat on
his head.

He is putting his hat on
his head.

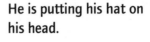

He put his hat on
his head.
He put it on.

It was on the table.
It is on his head.

He will take his hat off
his head.

He is taking his hat off
his head.

His hat is in his hand.
It was on his head.

He took his hat off.

It is in his hand.

This is a hat.

These are hats.

This is a hand.

These are hands.

This is a table.

These are tables.

This is a man.

These are men.

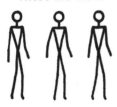

This is a woman.

These are women.

This is a man.

 This is
his hand.

It is the man's hand.

This is a woman.

 This is
her hand.

It is the woman's hand.

This is a man's hat.
It is on a man's head.

Now it is in the man's hands.
It is in his hands.

This is a woman's hat.
It is on a woman's head.

Now it is in the woman's hands.
It is in her hands.

He will give his hat to the man.

He is giving his hat to the man.

He gave it to the man.
He gave it to him.

It is in the man's hands now.

The man will give his hat to the woman.

He is giving his hat to the woman.

He gave it to the woman.
He gave it to her.

It is in the woman's hands now.

The woman will put the hat on the table.

She is putting it on the table.

She put it there.

It was in her hand.
It is on the table.

This is a ship.

These are ships.

This ship is in the bottle.

These ships are on the water.

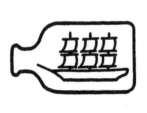

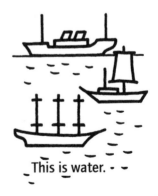

This is water.

This is water.

This is a bottle.

The bottle
is in a
man's hand.

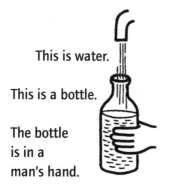

This is a glass.
It is on the table.

Now the glass is off the table.

The glass and the water are on the floor.

This is a bottle

and this
is a bottle.

This
and
this are bottles.

This is a glass

and this is
a glass.

These
are glasses.

That is a bird and
that is a bird.
Those are birds.
They are birds.

That man and that
woman are there.

This man and this
woman are here.

This is a man.

These are his arms.

These are his legs.

These are his feet.

This is an arm.

This is a leg.

This is a foot.

This is a table.

These are its legs.

Its feet are on the floor.

This is a seat.

These are its arms.

These are its legs.

Its feet are on the floor.

This is a room.

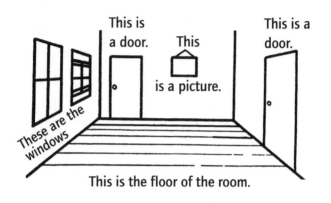

This is
a door.

This
is a picture.

This is a
door.

These are the windows

This is the floor of the room.

These are the windows of the room.

This is a window and this is a window.

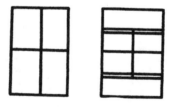

This window
is shut.

This window
is open.

This door is open.

This door is shut.

This is a wall of the room.

This
is a
wall.

A picture is on this wall.

This is the floor of the room.

This is a picture of a man and a woman.

This is the cord of the picture.

This is a hook.

This is the frame of the picture.

This is a house.

This is
a window
of the
house.

These are
windows
of the
house.

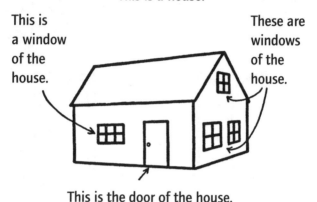

This is the door of the house.

These are houses.

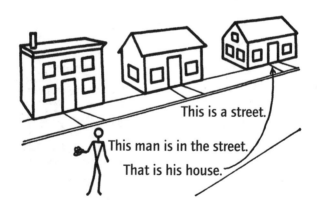

This is a street.

This man is in the street.

That is his house.

The man will
go to his house.

He
is going
to his house.

The man went
to his house.
He is there.

He went there.

He was here.

He is at his door.

He is at the door
of his house.

What is this?

This is a question mark.

It is a hat.
"What is this?" is a
question.
"It is a hat," is an answer.

We put question marks
after questions.

"Is this a hat?"
That is a question.
"Yes, it is."
That is an answer.

"Is this a hat?"
"No, it is not a hat. It is
a hand."
That is an answer.

a

What is this?
It is a _____

b

What is this?

c What is this?

d What is this?

e What is this?

f What is this?

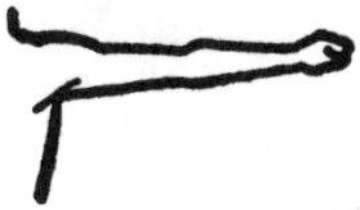

g What is this?

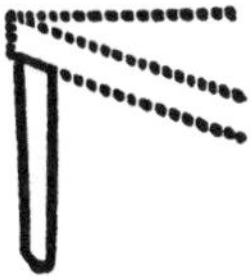

h What is this?

The answers are on page **34**.

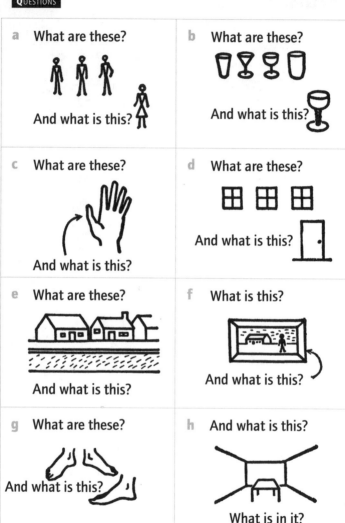

a What are these?

And what is this?

b What are these?

And what is this?

c What are these?

And what is this?

d What are these?

And what is this?

e What are these?

And what is this?

f What is this?

And what is this?

g What are these?

And what is this?

h And what is this?

What is in it?

The answers are on page **34**.

a Is the hat on the table?	**b** Is the man in the room? 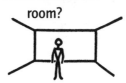
c Is the picture on the wall?	**d** Is the bird on the seat? 
e Is the glass in the woman's hand?	**f** Is the water in the glass?
g Is this ship in a bottle? 	**h** Are the man and the woman at the door? 

The answers are on page **34**.

Page 31

a It is a house.
b It is a ship.
c It is a table.
d It is a bottle.
e It is a leg.
f It is an arm.
g It is a leg of a table.
h It is an arm of a seat.

Page 32

a They are three men.
   That is a woman.
b They are glasses.
   That is a glass.
c They are fingers.
   That is the thumb.
d They are windows.
   That is a door.
e They are houses.
   That is a street.
f It is a picture of a man
   and a house.
   That is the frame of
   the picture. (Its frame)
g They are feet.
   That is a foot.
h That is a room.
   A table is in it.

Page 33

a Yes, it is.
b Yes, he is.
c No, it is not.
   It is on the floor.
d No, it is not.
   It is on the floor.
e No. It is in the man's
   hand.
f No, it is not in the glass.
g No. It is on the water.
h Yes, they are at the
   door.

What is this?
This is a clock.
What is the time?
The time is one (1:00).
One hand is at one.

What is the time?
The time is two (2:00).
It was one (1:00).
It will be three (3:00).

What is the time?
The time is four (4:00).
It was three (3:00).
It will be five (5:00).

What is the time?
Now the time is six (6:00).
It was five (5:00).
It will be seven (7:00).

What is the time?
Now the time is eight
(8:00).
It was seven (7:00).
It will be nine (9:00).

What is the time?
Now the time is ten
(10:00).
It was nine (9:00).
It will be eleven (11:00).

What is the time?
The time is twelve (12:00).
It was eleven (11:00).
It will be one (1:00).
The two hands are at
twelve now.

These are the numbers
from one to twelve.

One, two, three, four, five,
six, seven, eight, nine, ten,
eleven, twelve.

What are things?

A house is a thing.
Houses are things.

A hat is a thing. Hats are things.

Doors and windows are things.
Tables and seats are things.

This is a man.

This is a woman.

This is a boy.

This is a girl.

Men and women and boys and girls are not things. They are persons. You are a person.

There are two persons in this room.
They are a boy and a girl.

The girl is at the door.
The boy is at the window.

The girl will go to the window.

She will be with the boy at the window.
She will be with him at the window.

The girl is going to the window.
Where was she?

She was at the door.

She went to the window.
Where is she now?
She is at the window now.

She is with the boy.

They are at the window together.
She is with him at the window. He is with her at the window.

These books are together on the shelf.

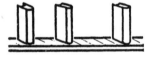

These books are not together. They are on the shelf, but they are not together.

The girl and the boy will go from the window.

They are going from the window. They were at the window.

They went from the window.
She went with him and he went with her.

Now they are at the door together.
The boy is with the girl at the door.
She is at the door again.

This is my head.

That is her head.

These are my eyes.

Her eyes are open.

This is one eye.

This is the other eye.

Her eyes are shut.

My eyes are open.
I see.
Her eyes are shut.
She does not see.

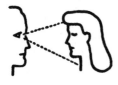

I see her.
She does not see me.

Now her eyes are open.
She sees.
What does she see?
She sees me.

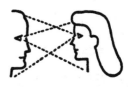

I see her.
Our eyes are open.

Her eyes are open.

She sees.
They were shut.
She did not see.

She did not see me.

Her eyes are shut.

They were open.
She saw.
What did she see?

She saw me.

A man has two eyes.
I have two eyes.

These are my eyes.

A man has a nose.
I have a nose.

This is my nose.

A man has a mouth.
I have a mouth.

This is my mouth.

This man's mouth is open.
He is saying "mouth."

His mouth is shut.

He is not saying "mouth."

His mouth is shut.
He will say "mouths."

He is saying "mouths."

He said "mouths."
He is not saying
"mouths" now.
His mouth is shut again.

These are three books.

They are on a shelf.

This book is between the other two books.

I have the book in my hand now.
It was on the shelf. It was between the other two books on the shelf.

These are the pages of the book.

These are the covers of the book.

The pages are between the covers of the book.

These are the fingers of my hand.

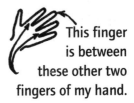This finger is between these other two fingers of my hand.

My nose is between my eyes.

And it is between my eyes and my mouth.

My mouth is under my nose.

My nose is over my mouth.
Our noses are over our mouths.

The light is over the table.

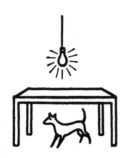

The dog is under the table.

This is a clock.

It is on the wall.
It is over the bookshelves.

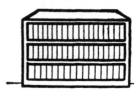

The bookshelves are under the clock.

This is his hair.
It is short.

This is her hair.
It is long.

These are his ears.

Where are her ears?
They are under
her hair.

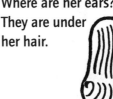

Her hair is over her ears.

This is his head.

This is his face.
His eyes, his nose, and
his mouth are parts of
his face.

This is a clock.

It has a face.
This is the face of the
clock. The clock has two
hands, a long hand and
a short hand. The long
hand is at 5. The short
hand is between 7 and 8.

A clock has a face.

It has no nose.

It has no eyes.

It has no mouth.

It has no ears.

It has no hair
but it has a face.

It has a face and two
hands, the long hand

and the short hand.

The long hand of the
clock is between one and
two.
One is before two. Two is
between one and three.
Three is after two and
two is after one.

I have this book in my
hands.
It was on the shelf with
the other books.
It was between the other
two books before I took
it from the shelf.

I have it in my hand.
I am putting it between
the other two books.
Then it will be with the
other books on the
bookshelf.

Now it is on the shelf
again. It was in my hand.
I had it in my hand. It is
not in my hand. Where
is it?

This is a room.
What do you see in the
room?
Do you see the floor and
three walls of the room?
Do you see them?

Do you see a door and
two windows?
Is one of the windows
open?
Is the other window shut?
Do you see two seats
and the bookshelves
between them?
Do you see the clock
over the bookshelves?
Yes. I see them.
These things are in the
room. The room is in
a house.

This is a face.

Eyes, nose, and mouth are parts of a face.

Which are the eyes?
Which is the nose?
Which is the mouth?

These are my hands.
Which is my right hand?
Which is my left hand?
Which are my thumbs?
Which are my fingers?

This is a man.
Which are his arms?
Which are his hands?
Which are his legs?
Which are his feet?

This is his head.

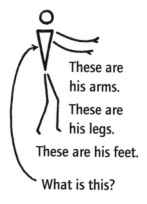

These are his arms.

These are his legs.

These are his feet.

What is this?

This is his body.

His head, his arms, his legs, and his body are parts of a man.

He has a body.

She has a body.

All men and women and boys and girls have bodies.

This baby has a body.

This dog has a body.
This is his tail.

This is his body.

He has four legs and a head and a tail. He has no arms or hands, but he has feet. His head, his body, his legs, and his tail are parts of a dog.

This is a dog's head.

Which is his mouth?
Which are his eyes?
Which are his ears?
Which is his nose?

This is a foot.

These are toes.
They are parts of a foot.
These parts of a foot are
its toes.

This is a toe.

This is a leg.

This is a knee.
It is part of a leg.

This part of a leg is
its knee.

Our legs are parts of us.

This is a neck.

It is a part of a man. It is
between his head and
his body.
The part which is
between his head and
his body is his neck.

This is a man's head.

This is his chin.
It is under his mouth.
It is a part of his face.
The part which is under
his mouth is his chin.

This is a man's body.

The part which is between his head, his arms, and his legs is his body.

This is his body.

This part of him is his chest.

This is a chest of drawers.

This man has his finger on his chin.

This man has his hand on his chest.

This baby is on his hands and knees.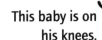

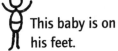

This baby is on his hands and feet.

This baby is on his knees.

This baby is on his feet.

Where is the dog?

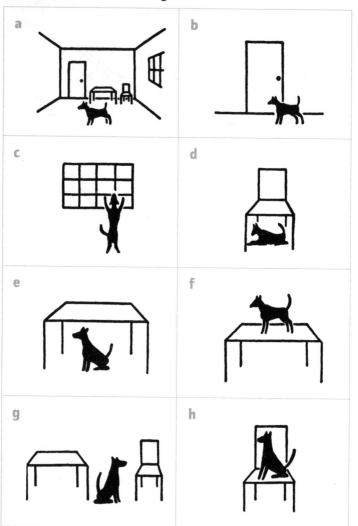

The answers are on page **56**.

QUESTIONS What do you see?

The answers are on page **56**.

What is he saying?

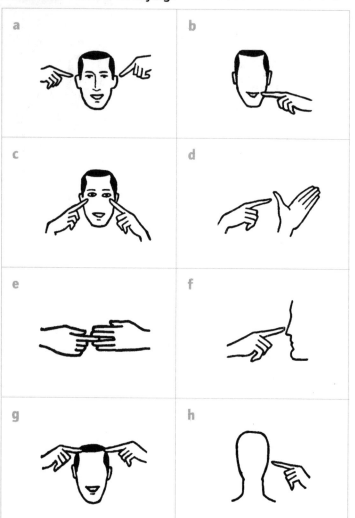

The answers are on page **57**.

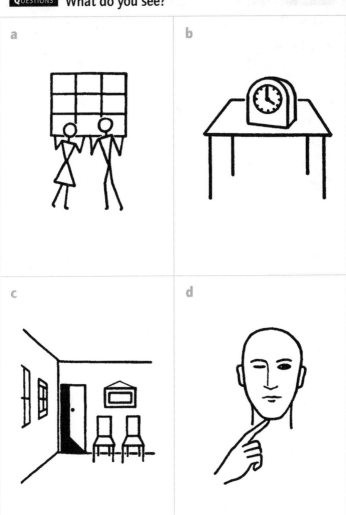

a

b

c

d

The answers are on page **57**.

Page 52

a The dog is in the room.

b The dog is at the door.

c The dog is at the window.

d The dog is under the chair.

e The dog is under the table.

f The dog is on the table.

g The dog is between the chair and the table.

h The dog is on the chair.

Page 53

a I see a clock.

b I see a man.

c I see a woman.

d I see a baby.

e I see two books.

f I see two girls and a book.

g I see two babies.

h I see a chest of drawers.

Page 54

a He is saying, "These are my ears."

b He is saying, "This is my mouth."

c He is saying, "These are my eyes."

d He is saying, "This is my thumb."

e He is saying, "This finger is between these fingers."

f He is saying, "This is my nose."

g He is saying, "This is my hair."

h He is saying, "This is my head."

Page 55

a I see a boy and a girl. They are at a window.

b I see a clock on a table. The time is four.

c I see a room. It has two seats in it. It has two windows and a door. One of the windows is open. The other window is shut. The door of the room is open. A picture is on the wall.

d I see a man. He has his finger on his chin. One of his eyes is open. The other eye is shut. His mouth is shut. He has no hair on his head.

Who is this?
He is John Smith.
His name is John Smith.
Where is John Smith?
He is at the door of his house.

He has his hand in his pocket.

He is taking a key from his pocket.

This is a key.

These are other keys.

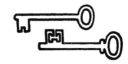

He will put the key in the lock of the door.

He is putting the key in the lock.

He is giving a turn to the key.

He is giving a push to the door.
The door is open now.

John took the key from the lock.
He is putting it in his pocket.
He will go into his house.

He is going into the house.

He went into the house.
He is in the house.
The door is shut.

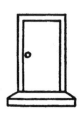

This is a room in the house.
Is John in the room?
No, he is not.

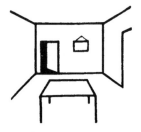

He will come into the room.

He is coming into the room.
He will go to the table.

Mr. Smith came into the room.
He went to the table.

Is Ms. Smith in the room?

She is in the house but she is not in the room.
She is in another room in the house.

No, she is not.

Who is this?
This is Mary Smith.
She is Ms. Smith.
Her name is Mary Smith.

This is one of the doors of the room.

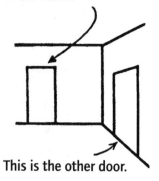

This is the other door.

This is one of the windows of the room.

This is another window.

And this is another window.
One window is open.
The other windows are shut.

This is one of my hands.
It is my left hand.

This is my other hand.
It is my right hand.

This is one of my fingers.

This is my left thumb.
These are the other fingers of my left hand.

Ms. Smith is not in the room.
She went out of the room.

She went through this door.

Mr. Smith is in the room.
He came into the room.

He came through this door.

Mr. Smith is putting his hat on the table.

He will go out of the room through this door.

He put his hat on the table.
It is on the table now.

He went out of the room through this door.

Mary is coming into the room.

She is going to the table.

She will see the hat.

She sees it.

She saw it.
When did she see it?
She saw it after she went
to the table.

She will take the hat in her hand.

She is taking it.

She took it in her hand. She is going out of the room.

She went out of the room with John's hat.

She has the hat in her hand.

She is in another room now.
She came into this room through this door.

She has the hat with her.

What are these?
They are hooks.

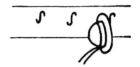

That is another hat.
It is on a hook.

She will put John's hat on a hook.

She will put it on a hook with the other hat.

She put it on the hook.

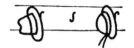

Now it is with the other hat.
The other hat is one of Mary's hats.

John is coming into the room again.

He came into the room.
He went to the table.

He is there now.

The hat is not on the table.

He is saying,

> Where is my hat?
> I put it on the table.

" Where is my hat? It is not on my head. It isn't here."

"It isn't (is not) here."

" Where is it? Mary, where is my hat? Where are you, Mary?"

Here is Mary. She is coming into the room. She says, "Here I am."

"Where is your hat?"

" You put it on the table.
It was on the table."

" I took it. I put it in the
other room."

" It is on a hook there.
You will see it there."

John says, "I will get my hat."

He is getting it.

Did he get it? Yes. He has it.

He went out of the room.

When he saw the hat he took it off the hook.

He came into the room again with the hat in his hands.
He got it.

He is giving the hat to Mary.

See what is in the hat, Mary!

What is in the hat?
Mary will see.

What is she taking from the hat?

What is that in her hand?
It is money.

Do you see?

She sees.

What does she see?
One thousand dollars.

The money is in
her hand.
It was in the hat.

Where was the hat?
It was on the table.

What did she see?
She saw the hat.
She did not see
the money.

She put the hat in the
other room.
John went there and
got it.

Who got it? John did.

Does she see the money
now?
Yes, she sees it.

Oh John! Where did
you get it?

I was in the street.
I was coming here.

The wind came. It took
my hat off.

I went after my hat.

When I took it up, there
was this money.

The money was under
the hat.

The hat was over the
money.

The wind came. My hat
went up.
When the wind came, my
hat went up.

The hat came down
again.

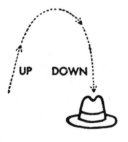

It was over the money.
The money was under
the hat.

What is Mary doing?

She is taking things from
a drawer.
What are those things in
the drawer?

Mary has a knife,
a fork and a spoon
in her right hand.

They are knives, forks and
spoons.

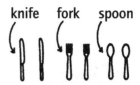

knife   fork   spoon

The drawer has knives,
forks and spoons in it.

She took them from
the drawer.
She will put them on
the table.

These are drawers.
One of them is open.
The other two drawers
are shut.

Mary is getting the soup.
These are plates of soup.

John is taking the seats
to the table.

Mary is in her seat at the
table.

John is in his seat.
They are in their seats
at the table.

Now they are taking their soup.

They have their spoons in their hands.

John is saying to Mary, "I took the hat up."

Mary is saying to John, "Where did the money come from?"

John said, "I saw it there under the hat."

Mary said, "But who put it there?"

John said, "Nobody put it there. The money was there and the wind came and put the hat down over the money."

Nobody = no man or woman or boy or girl or baby.

This dress is new.

This dress is old.

This pipe is new.

This pipe is old.

Mary is getting the new dress. She is in a store. The other woman has two dresses in her hands.

This is the store.

Dresses and hats and shoes are in the window of the store.

These are shoes.
They are women's shoes.

These are stockings.

These are gloves.
Dresses and stockings and shoes and gloves are clothing.

This is a tree.

This is a
branch
of the tree.
An apple
is on this
branch.
It is over
the girl's
head.

She will take the apple
from the branch.
She will put her hand up.

She put her
hand up.
She took the
apple. It is in
her hand.
She took the
apple which is
in her hand.
She has it in
her hand.
She is putting it
in her basket.

She put it in her basket.
She had it in her hand
before she put it in
her basket.
It was on the branch
before she put her hand
up and took it.

After she took the apple
she put it in the basket.
Then she put her basket
down. The apple was up
on the tree.
Now it is down in the
basket.

When was the apple on the branch?

When was it over her head?
It was on the branch before she took it. It was on the branch then.

When did she take it?

She took it after she put her hand up.
She took it then.

When did she put it in the basket?

She put it in the basket after she took it from the branch.

When did she have the apple in her hand?

She had it in her hand after she took it from the branch and before she put it in the basket.

This is a box.

This is the front
of the box.

This is the back of
the box.

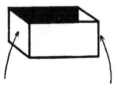

And these are the sides
of the box.

This is a house.

This is the front
of the house.
This is the front door.

This is a coat.

This is the front
of the coat.

These are the arms of
the coat.

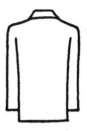

These are the sides of
the coat.

And this is the back of
the coat.

These are a man's arms.

These are his sides.

And this is his back.

Who is this?
This is Ms. Smith.
She is Mary Smith.
"Mary Smith" is
her name.

What is that? What is in
her hands?
It is a tray.
She has a tray in
her hands.

She will put the tray on
the table.

She is putting the tray on
the table.

She put the tray on the table.

It was in her hands.
It is on the table now.

Here is the tray.

What are these things on the tray?

These are glasses.

What are these?
They are forks.

What is this?
It is a knife.

What are these?
They are two other knives.

What are these?
They are spoons.

What is this?
It is another spoon.

What is this?
It is a plate.

These are three other plates.

Ms. Smith is taking a
knife and fork off
the tray.
She has them in
her hands.

She is putting them on
the table.

Now she is putting the
plates on the table.

She put the knives and
forks and spoons and
plates and glasses on
the table.
She put these things on
the table.

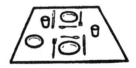

Mary Smith will go from the table to the door.

She is going to the door.
The door is shut.

She went out of
the room.
The door is open now.
It was shut.

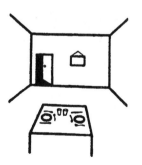

Mary Smith is not in
the room.
She was in the room.
She went out of the room.

What is this?
It is a knife.

What is this?

What is this?

What is this?

What are these?

What is this?

What is this?

What is this?

What is this?

What are these?

What is this?

What is this?

What are these things?

Mary is making soup.

This is a plate of soup.

She will make the soup from milk and potatoes.

These are potatoes.

This is a bottle of milk. It is cow's milk.

This is a cow.

Cows are animals.
These are some other animals.

a pig

a sheep

a horse

We get milk from cows. Mary is putting some milk in a cup.

The milk is going into the cup.

Mary has a potato in her hand.

She is taking its skin off with a knife.

We get potatoes from the roots of a plant.

Here they are in the earth.

We get them up with a fork.

This is a plant.
This is its flower.
These are its leaves.
These are its fruit.
This is a branch.
This is its stem.
These are its roots.

These are roots of other plants.

Mary is making the soup.

This is the pot.

This is the cover
of the pot.

She will make the soup
in this pot.

She put the potatoes in
the pot.
The water in the pot
is boiling.

This is a flame.

The pot is over the flame.
The flame is under
the pot.

This is steam.

This water is boiling.
It is giving off steam.
The heat of the flame is
making it give off steam.

Ice is solid.
This is ice.

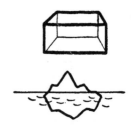

Water is a liquid.
This is water.

This is a tray.
It is a tray of ice.

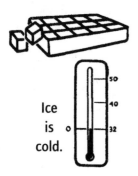

Ice
is
cold.

The room is warm.
The heat of the flame is
making the room warm.
The things in the room
are warm.
Ice is not warm.
It is cold.

80

This is a bird.
It is on a tree.

The other birds are
not on the tree.
They are in the air.

This is a plane.
It is in the air.
It is an airplane.
It is going through
the air.

These are airplanes.

We take in air through
our mouths and through
our noses.

The air comes in. Then it
goes out. That is a breath.

in out   one breath

in out
in out   two breaths

The air is coming
out. It is warm.
When it comes
out it is warm.

Put your hand
here. Your breath
is warm.

The room is warm.
The water in the pot is
very warm.
It is boiling.

212°
100°

The air over the flame is
very warm.
It goes up.

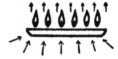

The air under the flame is
not very warm. It goes up
to the flame.

This is the icebox.
It has ice in it.
The air in the icebox
is cold.

This is   These are
milk.   eggs.

This is the icebox.
Mary keeps the milk in
the icebox.
She keeps it in the
cold air.
The air in the icebox
is cold.
The cold air keeps the
milk cold.

This is a clock.

A clock is an instrument for measuring time.

This is an instrument for measuring heat.

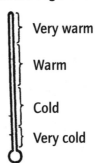

Very warm

Warm

Cold

Very cold

This is a measure.
It is a yard measure.

There are three feet in a yard.

There are twelve inches in a foot.

This is Mary's foot.

These are her feet.

This is John's foot.
It is ten inches long.

The walls and floor of the icebox are thick.

Warm air Cold air Warm air

This is a <u>thin line</u>.
This is a <u>thick line</u>.

The thick walls keep the heat of the room out of the icebox.
They keep the heat from the milk.
The cold air in the icebox keeps the milk good.

John is having a drink.
He is having a drink of milk from a glass.

This milk is not good.
It is bad.

The milk is good.
John is happy.

John is not happy.

This is meat.

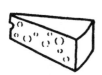

Mary keeps the meat in the icebox.

This is bread.

Mary does not keep the bread in the icebox. She keeps it in a bread-box.

This is cheese.

We make cheese from milk. We get milk from cows.

This is butter.

We make butter from milk. Mary keeps the butter with the milk in the icebox. She keeps the cheese there.

These are apples.

These are oranges.

Apples and oranges
are fruit.
Does Mary keep the fruit
in the icebox?

What is the time?

The time is five (5:00).
It is five.
Mary will make the soup.

What is the time?

It's five-thirty (5:30).
Mary is making the soup.
The potatoes are in the
pot. The water in the pot
is boiling.

It is five-forty (5:40).

Mary has a fork in
her hand.

She is putting the fork
into the potatoes.

The potatoes are hard.
The fork does not go
into them.

It is five-fifty (5:50).
Mary is putting the fork
in again.
She is doing it again.

The potatoes are soft.
The fork goes into them.

She is taking them out
of the pot and putting
them on a plate.

The potatoes are on the plate.

Mary is crushing them with a fork.

They were in the pot.
They were hard.
They are soft now.

They are not hard now.
They are soft.

Bread is soft.

Glass is hard.

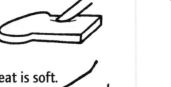

Meat is soft.

Butter is soft.

John has a bit of cheese
in his fingers.

He is putting the bit of
cheese in his mouth.

Now it is between
his teeth.

This is his mouth.

This is a tooth.

These are teeth.

The cheese is not soft.

It is hard.

John's teeth do not go
into the cheese.

Mary put the potatoes
and the milk and other
things into the pot.
This is salt.

She put the pot over a
low flame.
She put the cover on
the pot.

The low flame is under
the pot.

This flame is low.

This flame is high.

This building is high.

This building is low.

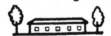

What is the time?
It is six (6:00).

Mary is tasting the soup.
It has a good taste.
The soup is ready.

Now she is putting the
soup in the plates.

It was in the pot.

Now it is in the plates.

She made the soup.
She put it in the plates.
She took them to
the table.

The plates are on
the table.
The soup is ready.
It is good soup.
Mary made it.

Soup, potatoes, milk, meat, bread, butter, cheese, apples, oranges

are food.

They are different sorts of food.

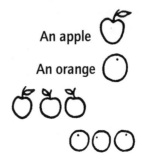

An apple

An orange

Apples and oranges are different sorts of fruit.

These are different sorts of glasses.

These are different sorts of boxes.

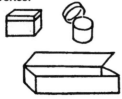

Glasses and boxes and fingers and dresses and flames are things. They are different sorts of things.

Cows

and sheep

and pigs

and horses

and goats
are animals.

They are different sorts
of animals.

These are different sorts
of plants.

This is the leaf of one
sort of plant.

This is the leaf of
another sort of plant.

These are the same.
O O O O O O

These are different.
△ ☐ ☆ O

These are the same.
O O

These are different.
o ○

These plates are
the same.

These plates are
different.

These glasses are
the same.

These are
different.

Here are a woman
and a boy.

The boy is the woman's
son.
She is his mother.
He is her son.

Here are a woman
and a girl.

The girl is the woman's
daughter.
The woman is her
mother.

Here are a man and
his son.

The man is the father of
the boy.
He is the boy's father.

Here are a man and
his daughter.

He is the father
of the girl.
He is the girl's father.
She is his daughter.

The boy is the brother of the girl.

He is the girl's brother.
He is her brother.

The girl is the sister of the boy.
She is the boy's sister.
She is his sister.

This man and woman

have two sons

and three daughters.

This boy has one brother and three sisters.
This girl has two brothers and two sisters.
They are a family of seven (7).

Here are Ms. Smith,
her daughter Jane, and
her son Tom.

They are at the table.
They are having their
potato soup.

Potato soup is a thick
soup. It is not clear.
Thick soup and clear
soup are two different
sorts of soup.

This water
is clear.
When a
liquid is
clear we see
through it.

Milk is not a
clear liquid.
We do not
see through it.

The air is clear. I see
the mountains.
When the air is not clear
I do not see them.

This soup is clear.
We see the spoon
through it.
Potato soup is a thick
soup. We do not see the
spoon through it.

Who is this?

This is Mary Smith.
She made the soup.
This is Mary who made
the soup.

This is the soup. Mary
made it.
This is the soup which
Mary made.

This is the milk.
Mary put it in
the soup.
This is the milk which
Mary put in the soup.

This is a spoon. It is in my hand.
This is a spoon which is in my hand.

That is a glass of water. It is on the table.
That is a glass of water which is on the table.

This is a bone. It was in the dog's mouth.
This is a bone which was in the dog's mouth.

This is a dog. He had the bone.

This is the dog who had it.

a What is the time?

b What are these?

c What is this?

d What are these?

e What are these?

f What is this?

g What is this?

h What is this?

The answers are on page **116**.

a What is this?

b What is this?

c What are these?

d What is this?

e What is this?

f What is this?

g What is this?

h What is this?

The answers are on page **116**.

a This is a family.

What do you see?

b This is a plant.

Which parts of the plant do you see?

c This is an icebox.

What do you see in it?

d This is a dog.

Which parts of the dog do you see?

e What do you see?

f What do you see?

g What do you see?

h What do you see?

The answers are on page **116**.

Page 113

a The time is three-forty-two (3:42).

b They are apples.

c It is a pot.

d They are leaves.

e They are roots.

f It is a bottle of milk.

g It is butter.

h It is bread.

Page 114

a It is cheese.

b It is a cup.

c They are flames.

d It is a horse.

e It is a high building.

f They are a box and its cover.

g It is a pig.

h It is a sheep.

Page 115

a I see a father and mother and their son and daughter.

b I see its roots and its stem and its leaves and its flower.

c I see a bottle of milk and four eggs and two roots.

d I see its head and ears and nose, its body, its legs, and its tail.

e I see a bone. It is on the floor. And I see the leg of a table.

f I see two glasses. One of them has liquid in it.

g I see a woman. She has a spoon in her hand. She is tasting the soup.

h I see a man. He has a glass in his hand. He is having a drink from the glass.

a Where are the women?

What does one woman have in her hands?

b What are these?

c What is the girl doing?

Where is the apple?

d

Where will she put the apple?
Where was it before she took it?
(See pages 82-83)

e

What are some different sorts of food?

f

What are some different sorts of animals?

g

What are some different sorts of fruits?

h

What are some different sorts of persons?

The answers are on page **120**.

a This is a glass of milk.
Is it clear? Do you see through it?

b Is the glass in this window clear?
What do you see through the window?

c Is glass hard?

d Is meat soft?

e Is ice warm?

f Are flames cold?

g What is he doing?

h What is she doing?

The answers are on page **121**.

a What do you see?

b What is he doing?

c What are they doing?

d What are these?

e What do we keep in the icebox?

f What are some different sorts of things? Give the names of ten different things which you see in a house.

The answers are on page **121**.

Page 117

a They are in a store. It
   is a clothing store.
   She has two dresses in
   her hands.

b These are shoes
   (women's shoes) and
   stockings and gloves.

c The girl is putting her
   hand up to the apple.
   It is on a branch of an
   apple tree.

d She will put it in her
   basket. Before she took
   the apple it was on
   the tree.

e Bread, butter, milk,
   cheese, meat, eggs, and
   fruit are different sorts
   of food.

f Cows, pigs, sheep,
   goats, and horses
   are different sorts of
   animals.

g Apples and oranges
   are different sorts
   of fruit.

h Men, women, boys,
   girls, and babies
   are different sorts of
   persons.

Page 118

a No, it is not clear. No, I do not see through it.

b Yes. The glass in the window is clear. I see some mountains and a house.

c Yes. Glass is hard.

d Yes. Some meat is soft. But some meat is hard.

e No. Ice is cold.

f No. Flames are not cold.

g He is taking potatoes out of the earth with a fork.

h She is putting some salt in the potato soup.

Page 119

a I see a man. He is in a street. His hat is in the air. The wind is taking it up. The wind took it off his head.

b He is putting his hat on his head.

c They are in their seats at the table. They have their spoons in their hands. They are taking their soup.

d One of them is a clock. The other is an instrument for measuring heat.

e We keep the milk, butter, cheese, eggs, meat, and fruit in the icebox.

f Rooms and doors and windows and tables and seats and boxes and knives and spoons and forks and shelves... are different sorts of things.

A FIRST WORKBOOK OF ENGLISH

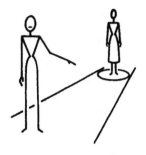

I am here.

She is there.

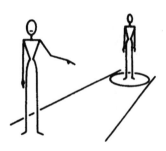

He is there.

He is here.

He is there.
She is there

He is here.
I am here.

1. _She is here._   2. _____

3. _____   4. _____

They are there.
It is there.

She is here.
They are here.

5. _____   6. _____

7. _____   8. _____

You are there.   They are here.
We are here.   You are here.

This is a ___hat___.

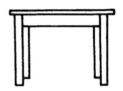

A **1** This is a _____.

2 This is a _____.

3 This is the _____.

4 These are the _____.

B 1 This a ___*man*___ is here.

He _____ here.

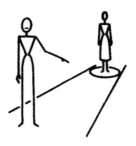

2 That woman is _____.

_____ is there.

This is a (<u>hat</u>, head, hand).

1 This is (his, her, my) hat.

2 That is your (left, right, the) hand.

3 (Her, His, Its) hat is on her head.

4 His hat is (in, my, on) his hand.

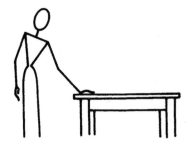

5 His hand is on his
(finger, head, thumb).

6 His hand is (in, here, on)
the table.

He _will put_ his hat on.

1 He is _____ his hat off.
  It _____ on his head.

2 She _____ her hat on the table.
  It _____ on the table.

3 She _____ her hat on.
It _____ in her hand.

4 He _____ his hat off the table.
It _____ on his head.

A 1 These are ___hands___.

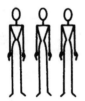

2 These are _____.

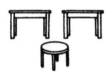

3 _____ are tables.

4 These are _____.

B 1 This <u>man's</u> hat is in _____ hand.

2 This _____ hat is on _____ head.

3 These _____ men's hats.

4 These are _____ hats.

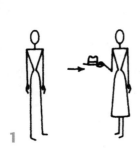

1

2

3

4

_____4_____	She is putting her hat on.
_____	These are bottles.
_____	He gave his hat to her.
_____	The ship is on the water.

5

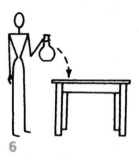

6

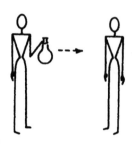

7

8

_____ He will put the bottle on the table.

_____ She is taking it off the table.

_____ He is putting the hat on the table.

_____ He will give the bottle to him.

1 The bottle is ___*in*___ a man's hand. (in, on)

2 The glass is _____ the table. (in, on)

3 _____ are glasses. (This, These)

4 Now the glass is off the table. _____
   is on the floor. (It, She)

5 That man and that woman are _____.
   (here, there)

6 This man and this woman are _____.
   (here, there)

7 That is a bird and that is a bird.
   _____ are birds. (Those, This)

8 That is a bird and that is a bird.
   _____ are birds. (You, They)

9 This is a man. _____ are his feet.
   (That, These)

10 That is a seat. Those are _____ legs.
   (its, his)

11 That is _____ arm and that is _____ leg.
   (a, an)

12 His _____ are on the floor. (foot, feet)

This is a r _o_ o _m_ .

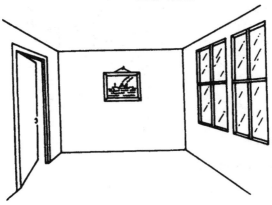

This is the f_l_oo_r_ of the r_o_om.

1 T___o ___i___d___w___ are in a ___al___.

2 ___h___y are s___u___.

3 The ___oo___ of the r___o___ is o___e___.

4 A ___i___t___re is on a ___a___l.

5 It is a ___ ___c___u___e of a s___i___.

6 The ___h___p is on the w___t___r.

7 The p___c___u___e is in a f___a___e.

8 It is on a ___o___d.

9 The c___r___ is on a ___o___k.

10 The h___o___ is in a ___al___.

1 This woman is in the ___street___.
   She _____ go to her house.

2 That _____ her house.
   She is _____ to her house.

3 The woman _____ to her house.
  She _____ at her house.
  She _____ in the street.

4 Now the woman is _____ the door
  _____ her house.
  The door is _____.
  The window is _____.

<u>What is this</u> is a question. We put a question mark after it: <u>What is this?</u> You will put question marks after the questions here:

1 Is this a house.
2 These are ships.
3 This is a hand.
4 What is that.
5 Is this a table.
6 No, it is not.
7 What are these.
8 The man will go to his house.
9 Yes, these are houses.
10 What is this.
11 This is a bird.
12 The woman went to her house.
13 She is at the door of the house.
14 Is that a picture.
15 This is a window of the house.
16 What is a question.

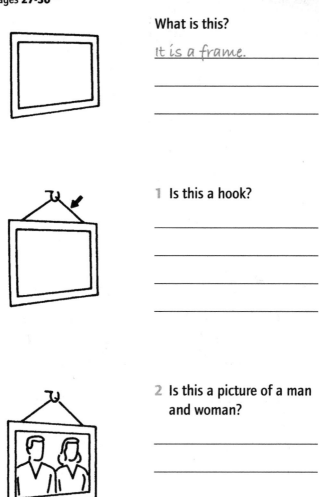

What is this?

It is a frame.

_____

_____

1 Is this a hook?

_____

_____

_____

_____

2 Is this a picture of a man
and woman?

_____

_____

_____

_____

1 What is the time?

It is _three_ .

It was _two_ .

It will be _four_ .

2 What is the time?

It is _____ .

It was _____ .

It will be _____ .

3 What is the time?

It is _____ .

It was _____ .

It will be _____ .

4 It was nine on this
clock.
It will be eleven.
What is the time?
It is _____.
Here is a picture of
the clock:

5 It was four.
It will be six.
What is the time?
It is _____.
You will put a picture
of the clock here:

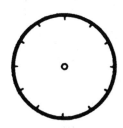

6 It was seven.
It will be nine.
What is the time?
It is _____.
You will put a picture
of the clock here:

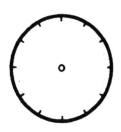

A 1 This is a _man_ .

He is a _person_ .

(person, thing)

2 This is a _____ .

It is a _____ .

(person, thing)

3 This is a _____ .

She is a _____ .

(person, thing)

4 This is a _____ .

It is a _____ .

(person, thing)

B 1 This is a girl. Is she a person?
You will put the answer here:

_____

_____

2 This is a boy. Is he a thing?
You will put the answer here:

_____

_____

1 The boy is in the street. The girl is in the house.
   They (are, <u>are not</u>) together.

2 Tom and Mary are together.
   Mary (is, is not) with Tom.

3 John is in his room.
   Mary is at the door of the house.
   John (is, is not) with Mary.
   They (are, are not) together.

4 The boy went the table together.
   The girl went to the table.
   They (are, are not) at the table together.

5 The bottle is on the table.
   The glass is on the shelf.
   The bottle and the glass (are, are not) together on
   the table.

6 Tom and Jane were in the street together.
   Tom (was, was not) with Jane.
   Jane (was, was not) with Tom.

She does not see me.   He did not see.

It is not open.   I see.

I am saying "nose."   She sees.

My eyes are open.

_____I see._____

A 1 My mouth is open.

_____

2 Her eyes are shut.

_____

3 Her eyes are open.

_____

4 His eyes were shut.

_____

5 His mouth is shut.

_____

B 1 Her ___eyes___ are

___shut___.

2 _____eyes

_____open.

3 _____ eye

_____ shut.

4 _____ eyes
are _____.

5 _____ is
_____ "open."

6 _____ sees
the _____.

A 1 The clock is __on__ the wall __over__ the seat.

2 The bottle is _____ the shelf _____
the picture.

3 It is _____ the book and the glass.

4 The feet _____ the dog are _____ the floor.

5 One hand _____ the clock is _____ twelve.

B **1** What is under the clock?

A seat is under the clock.

2 What is on the table?

3 Are the dogs feet on the seat?

4 What numbers are between four and seven on the clock?

5 What are the things on the shelf?

1 The short hand is between nine and ten.

2 _____

3 _____

4 _____

There is no long hand.
The short hand is between nine and ten.
The short hand is at four.
The long hand is at six.

5 _____

6 _____

7 _____

8 _____

It has a face.
Her ears are under her hair.
It has no eyes or ears.
Her hand is over a part of her face.

seven	eight	nine	ten
between	after	before	part

1 Eight is ___before___ nine.

2 Seven is _____ nine.

3 Nine is _____ eight.

4 Ten is _____ seven.

5 Eight is _____ seven and nine.

6 _____ is after nine.

7 _____ is before eight.

8 _____ and _____ are
between seven and ten.

9 Page seven is _____ page eight in
a book.

10 Page ten is _____ page nine.

11 Page eight is _____ pages seven
and nine.

12 A page is a _____ of a book.

<u>again</u>   <u>then</u>   <u>other</u>   <u>them</u>   <u>do</u>

Mary has two books in her hands. __Do__ you see them?
One is in her left hand and the _____ is in her
right. The two books were on the shelf before Mary
took _____ off. Mary will give the books to Tom.
He will put them on the shelf. _____ there will
be two books on the shelf _____.

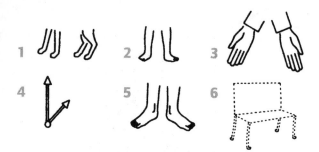

Which are the man's feet?

The man's feet are number 5.

A **1** **Which are the feet of the seat?**

_____

2 **Which are the baby's feet?**

_____

3 **Which are the dog's feet?**

_____

4 **Which are the man's hands?**

_____

5 **Which are the hands of the clock?**

_____

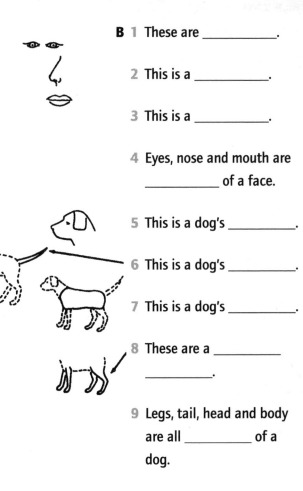

B 1 These are _____.

2 This is a _____.

3 This is a _____.

4 Eyes, nose and mouth are
_____ of a face.

5 This is a dog's _____.

6 This is a dog's _____.

7 This is a dog's _____.

8 These are a _____
_____.

9 Legs, tail, head and body
are all _____ of a
dog.

10 Windows, doors and walls
are parts of a _____.

1 Is a knee a part of a leg?

  Yes, it is a part of a leg.

---

2 Is a toe a part of a hand?

---

3 Are our necks parts of our faces?

---

4 Where is your chin?

---

5 Is a chest of drawers a thing?

---

6 Is a chest a part of a body?

_____

_____

7 Are your eyes parts of your face?

_____

_____

8 Is your nose over your eyes?

_____

_____

9 Are your ears parts of your head?

_____

_____

10 What is the part of a man which is between his
head, his arms and his legs?

_____

_____

This man is Mr. Wilson. His name is Jim Wilson. He is at the door of his house. He is putting his hand in his pocket. His door key is in that pocket. He will take the key from his pocket and put it in the lock of the door.

The door is shut now but it will be open. Mr. Wilson will give a turn to the key and a push to the door. Ms. Wilson is in the house. She will see him and then she will come to the door. He will take his hat off. She will put her hand in his. Then they will go into the house together and the door will be shut again.

1 What is the name of the man?

The man's name is Jim Wilson.

2 Where is he putting his hand?

_____

_____

3 What will he take from his pocket?

_____

_____

4 Where will he put his key?

_____

_____

5 Will he give a push to the key or to the door?

_____

_____

6 Is the door shut or open now?

_____

7 Who will come to the door?

_____

8 Will Mr. Wilson take his hat or his hands off?

_____

_____

9 Will he take Ms. Wilson's hand in his?

_____

_____

10 Where will they go together?

_____

<u>one</u>　　　<u>another</u>　　　<u>other</u>　　　<u>others</u>

1 That is ___one___ of his hands and that is
   the _____.
2 That is one wall of the room, that is _____,
   and those are the _____.
3 The _____ two walls have pictures on
   them.
4 She took _____ of my hands and then
   she took the _____.
5 _____ of the three windows was shut
   but the _____ were open.
6 Ms. Jones was out and the man said, "I will come
   again _____ time."
7 _____ of his fingers was short but the
   _____ were not.
8 _____ hand of the clock was long and
   the _____ was short.
9 He put _____ book on the shelf and
   took _____ one from it.
10 Mary went from _____ room to_____.

into   <u>into</u>   <u>to</u>   <u>in</u>   <u>out</u>   <u>of</u>   <u>at</u>

A 1 The man is _____*at*_____ the door of his house.

  2 He will go _____ his house from the street.

  3 Now he is _____ a room in his house.

  4 He will come _____ the house into the street again.

  5 He will go _____ the door of another house.

<u>is coming</u>   <u>came</u>   <u>are going</u>   <u>went</u>   <u>will go</u>

B   A woman _*is coming*_ out of the other house with a girl. She _____ out into the street with the girl. She _____ to another street. They _____ to the other street. They _____ to the other street and they are there now.

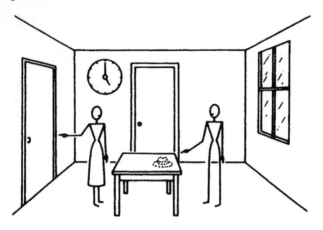

John and Mary are in the room. John says, "Where is my hat, Mary? It isn't on the table."

Mary says, "When did you put it on the table?"

John says, "I put it on the table before I went out. I went out at three. It is five now."

Mary says, "I came into the room at four and put your hat in another room. It is there now."

1 When did John put his hat on the table?

He put his hat on the table before

he went out.

2 Is John's hat on the table?

3 Where did Mary put John's hat?

4 Did Mary come into the room at four?

5 When did John go out of the room?

He is (get, <u>getting</u>, got) his book from the other room.

1 He (take, took, taking) the picture off the hook.

2 Do you (seeing, saw, see) what is on the floor?

3 She will (gave, give, giving) the key to him.

4 Did she (taking, took, take) the money from her pocket?

5 He is (go, going, went) out of the room.

6 We (putting, puts, put) the books on the shelf.

7 She will (come, coming, came) into the house.

8 Will she (going, went, go) out of the house?

9 He (says, say, saying), "Where is my key?"

10 He (seeing, see, sees) what is under the table.

11 He took it (when, again, did) he saw it.

12 (Did, What, Where) he get it?

What	Was	There	When	Does

Did	Who	Is	Will	Are	Do	Where

___Do___ we put our hats on in the house?

1 _____ the man in the street when the wind took his hat off?

2 _____ is the man doing?

3 _____ he going after his hat now?

4 _____ the wind came, did the hat go up?

5 _____ the wind take the hat up before it came down?

6 _____ a thing which goes up come down again?

7 _____ the money be in the man's hands?

8 _____ put the money under the hat?

9 _____ was the money when the hat was over it?

10 _____ dollars money?

Ms. Jones is not in the room. She was in the room. She took knives and forks and spoons out of one of the drawers of the chest and put them on the table. Then she went out of the room.

Now Mr. Jones is coming into the room. He is taking his hat off. He will put his hat on a hook on the door. He says, "Alice! Where are you, Alice?"

What is Alice doing? She is getting the soup. Here she is, coming into the room. There are two plates of soup in her hands. Alice Jones will put the soup on the table. She sees Tom's hat on the door.

Alice says, "Oh, there you are, Tom. Will you get the seats?"

Now Alice is taking her seat at the table. Tom is putting two glasses of water on the table. He will take his seat with Alice at the table. They will be in their seats at the table together.

Where were the knives and forks and spoons which Alice put on the table?

They were in a drawer of
the chest.

1 **What was Alice Jones doing when Tom Jones came in?**

2 **Was it Tom who put his hat on a hook on the door?**

3 **What was in the plates in Alice's hands?**

4 **Who put the glasses of water on the table?**

5 **Did Alice take her seat at the table after Tom?**

<u>from a clothing store</u>

<u>in her hand</u>   <u>in his mouth</u>

<u>of a leg</u>   <u>on his feet</u>

A **1** She is getting a new dress _from a clothing_

_store._____.

2 He has a pipe _____

_____.

3 She has her glass _____

_____.

4 He is putting his shoes _____

_____.

5 A knee is a part _____

_____.

<u>under the table</u>

<u>with a spoon</u>   <u>at a store</u>

<u>over the store</u>   <u>on her hands</u>

B 1 You get hats, stockings and shoes _____

_____.

2 We take soup _____

_____.

3 She is putting her gloves _____

_____.

4 There is nobody in the room _____

_____.

5 The dog is _____

_____.

Pages **80-81**

This is a new ___pipe___.

1 These are _____.

2 These are _____.

3 This is a _____ shoe.

4 This is a _____.

5 These are _____.

6 These are _____.

7 These are old _____.

8 This is an _____ hat.

A Mary took the book off the table. Then she gave it to John. John put it between the other two books on the shelf.

   1 Mary took the book off the table (after, <u>before</u>) she gave it to John.

   2 John put it on the shelf (after, before) he got it from Mary.

B Knives and forks and spoons were in the drawer. Alice took these things out of the drawer. She put them on the table. Then she went out of the room.

   1 Alice put knives and forks and spoons on the table (after, before) she took them out of the drawer.

   2 She put the knives and forks and spoons on the table (after, before) she went out of the room.

C The apple is in Mary's hand. It was on the branch of the tree. When Mary saw it, she took it from the branch. She will put it in the basket which she put down under the tree.

   1 The apple (which, when) was on the branch is in Mary's hand.

   2 Mary took it from the branch (which, when) she saw it.

Who is that man putting his coat on? What is his name?
That is Tom Jones. Tom Jones is the man's name. He has
his left arm in his coat and he is putting the other one
in. You see the back of his head and the back of his coat.
You do not see Alice Jones. She is in the street. She has a
box in her arms. Her arms are on the two sides of the
box and her hands are in front of it.

Tom will come out of the front door of the house when
he has his coat on. After the door is shut, he will put the
key in his pocket. Then he will take the box from Alice.

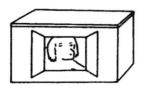

The box has a cover and a window in the front of it. There is a baby dog in the box.

_____Who_____ is that man?

1 _____ is his name?

2 The man's _____ is Tom Jones.

3 Tom is _____ his coat on.

4 He put his _____ arm in his _____ before his right _____.

5 Alice Jones is in the _____ with a _____ in her arms.

6 The box has a _____ and a window in the _____.

7 Tom will _____ the box when the _____ is shut and the _____ is in his pocket.

8 There is a _____ dog in the _____.

JANE AND HER BOY

Jane came _____ of the room. She had a tray in her _____. There _____ spoons and soup plates on the _____. She _____ the tray on a table. Then she _____ two cups off the shelf and went into the room.

Jane's boy, Jimmie, was _____ the floor with _____ open book. There was a picture _____ a potato _____ the page. He was saying, "What _____ this?"

Jane said, "That is a _____. You had potatoes in your _____. I make that soup from potatoes _____ milk."

Jimmie _____, "That is a potato." Then he put his finger _____ a picture on _____ page. "_____ is this?" said Jimmie.

"This is a cow," said Jane. "We _____ milk from cows."

"_____ get milk from a bottle," said Jimmie.

"Yes, but a man _____ the milk from a cow. _____ he puts it in _____," said Jane.

Jimmie put his _____ on another picture.

"_____ that a cow?" he said.

"_____," said Jane, "that is a horse and _____ is a pig and that _____ a sheep. Cows and horses and pigs and sheep are _____."

Jane _____ a bottle of milk off the table and put _____ milk in a cup.

She _____ the cup to Jimmie. "Here is your milk, Jimmie," _____ said.

"Where _____ we _____ milk?"

"We get milk _____ a cow," said Jimmie.

"Yes," said Jane. "Cows give _____ to us."

You will make these into questions:

This is an apple.

 Is this an apple?

1 The woman will put the cover on the pot.

2 The water in the pot was boiling.

3 An apple is a fruit.

4 She took the skin off the potato.

5 The roots of a plant go down into the earth.

6 There were no flowers on the plants.

_____

_____

7 These are leaves of a plant.

_____

_____

8 When water is boiling it gives off steam.

_____

_____

9 There is a flame under the pot.

_____

_____

10 A flower has a stem.

_____

_____

Here are a tray of water and a pot of water. When we make the water in the tray cold, it is turned into ice. When we put water in a pot over a flame some of it is turned into steam. The heat of the flame makes the water give off steam. Steam is not solid. Ice is solid. Water is a liquid.

A 1 What is water turned into when we make it cold in a tray?

_____

2 What makes water in a pot over a flame give off steam?

_____

3 Is steam solid?

_____

4 Is ice solid?

_____

5 Is water solid?

_____

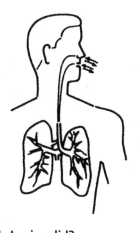

Air is not solid and it is not a liquid. We do not see it. Air which we take in and give out through our noses and mouths is our breath. The air which we give out is warm air.

B 1 Is air solid?

_____

2 Is air a liquid?

_____

3 Do we see air?

_____

4 What is our breath?

_____

5 Is the air which we give out warm air?

_____

In this picture you see a girl at a window in an airplane. The plane is over 10,000 feet up in the air. The air up there is cold. When the plane was going up the girl saw some birds in the air. She saw them through the window of the plane. Now she sees other airplanes but there are no birds up there.

C 1 Where is the girl in the picture?

_____

2 Is the plane up in the air?

_____

3 Is the air up there warm?

_____

4 What does the girl see through the window of the plane?

_____

5 Do birds go 10,000 feet up in the air?

_____

In this picture you see a girl at a window. The glass of the window is cold but the girl's breath is warm. It is turning to water on the cold window. The glass of the window in front of the girl's mouth has steam from her breath on it. She is making a mark on it with her finger. She will put her name on the window.

D 1 Where is the girl in the picture?

_____

2 Is the glass of the window cold?

_____

3 Is the girl's breath turning to water on the cold glass of the window?

_____

4 Is there steam on the glass of the window in front of the girl's mouth?

_____

5 What is the girl doing?

_____

1 A clock is an (<u>instrument</u>, inch) for measuring time.

2 There are three feet in a (yard, foot).

3 The book on the shelf is six (feet, inches) long.

4 When you get (eggs, milk) from a store there are twelve in a box.

5 An egg box is a box (for, of) eggs.

6 Mary (keeps, takes) her money in a drawer in her room.

7 A yard (measure, measuring) is three feet long.

8 (Measuring, Getting) a man's foot gives us the number of inches it is long.

9 A man's foot is (long, short) when it is over twelve inches.

10 The air over a flame is (very, not) warm.

1 We keep (<u>meat</u>, books) in the icebox.

2 We put butter on (bread, oranges).

3 We make (cheese, potatoes) from milk.

4 We take the skin off (oranges, bread) with a knife.

5 Milk is a good (drink, glass) for a baby.

6 When the milk in her glass is (good, bad) the girl is happy.

7 A book which has one thousand pages is a (thin, thick) book.

8 When his bottle of milk is bad the baby is (happy, not happy).

9 When (butter, an egg) is in the warm air it is soft.

10 A book which has twelve pages is a (thin, thick) book.

11 A girl who has a new dress is (happy, not happy).

12 The cheese is very old. It is (hard, soft).

13 The milk was in the warm air a long time. It is (good, bad) now.

14 When the short hand of a clock is between five and six and the long hand is at six it is (five-thirty, five-forty).

15 The potatoes were in boiling water a long time. They are (soft, hard) now.

Pages **100-105**

You will give answers to these questions:

1 Are eggs in an egg box ready for the table?

No, eggs in an egg box are not ready for the table.

2 Is some cheese hard?

3 Are all flames low?

4 Are all buildings high?

5 Is an orange a root or a fruit?

6 Does good soup have a good taste?

_____

_____

7 When do we see that potatoes in a pot are soft?

_____

_____

8 Is warm butter soft?

_____

_____

9 When we have an icebox do we keep the milk in it?

_____

_____

10 What keeps the heat from the things in an icebox?

_____

_____

OTHER   BUT   ONE   IS
BUILDINGS   THESE   HIGH
IS   OF   NOT   THE

1   _One of these buildings is high but_

the other is not.

TEETH   THE   HAS   BOY
CHEESE   OF   A   BIT
HIS   BETWEEN

2   _____

_____

IS   FORK   MS.   A
POTATOES   CRUSHING
THE   WITH   JONES

3   _____

_____

SOUP THE IS WOMAN
THE TASTING

4 _____

_____

HARD SOFT BUT
GLASS IS BUTTER IS

5 _____

_____

ORANGE OFF MARY
TAKING THE AN
PLATE IS

6 _____

_____

food   different   sorts   the same   sort

Sheep and goats are _different_ sorts of animals.

1 Apples and oranges are

_____ _____

of fruit.

2 Two of these plates are

_____ and one is

_____.

3 This is the leaf of one _____

_____ of plant.

4 These are _____ sorts of glasses.

5 These two glasses are _____

_____.

6 These two are _____.

7 Meat, cheese and milk are different sorts of _____.

___Which___ is a clear liquid, water or milk?

It is __water__ __which__ is a clear liquid.

1 _____ is soft, butter or glass?

It is _____ _____ is soft.

2 _____ apple did she take?

She took the _____ _____
was on the table.

3 _____ book will you have?

I will have the _____ _____
is in your left hand.

4 _____ of these two pipes will you give
to him?

I will give the_____ _____
is new to him.

5 _____ of these hats is yours?

The _____ _____ has the
bird on it is my hat.

6 _____ house was his house?

The _____ _____ has six
windows was his.

THE GREEN FAMILY

1 Mr. and Mrs. Green have two __boys__ and
   one __girl__.

2 The Greens are a _____ of five.

3 The _____ of the boys and the girl is
   Mr. Joe Green.

4 Mary Green (Mrs. Joe Green) is their _____.

5 Lucy Green is the _____ of Mr. and
Mrs. Green.

6 Their _____ are Tom and John.

7 Towser is their dog but he is not one of the
Green _____.

8 Tom and John are Lucy's _____.

9 Lucy is their _____.

10 Joe and Mary are the _____ and
_____ of John, Tom and Lucy.

This is a boy. He went to the store.

This is the boy who went to
the store .

This is a hat. It was on a hook.

This is the hat which was on
a hook.

1 **That is a man. He was on the mountain.**

_____

_____

2 **This is cheese. It was in the icebox.**

_____

_____

3 **This is Ms. Jones. She put the cheese in the icebox.**

_____

_____

4 **This is milk. John got it.**

_____

_____

5 This is potato soup. Mary made it.

_____

_____

6 That is water. It is clear.

_____

_____

7 This is a bone. It was in the dog's mouth.

_____

_____

8 This is a spoon. It was in Tom's hand.

_____

_____

9 This is Jane. She came to our house.

_____

_____

10 This is a dog. He had a bone in his mouth.

_____

_____

The i in icebox and the i in line are the same. The i
in thick and the i in high are different.

1 Is i the same in these: line, high?

   Yes, the i is the same.

   _____

2 Are the o's in low and soft the same or different?

   _____

   _____

3 Are the a's in bad and salt the same or different?

   _____

   _____

4 Are the o's in coat and bone the same or different?

   _____

   _____

5 Are the a's in says and wall the same or different?

   _____

   _____

6 Are the i's in thin and drink the same or different?

   _____

   _____

7 Are the <u>a</u>'s in <u>yard</u> and <u>hard</u> the same or different?

_____

_____

8 Are the <u>u</u>'s in <u>butter</u> and <u>crushing</u> the same or different?

_____

_____

9 Are the <u>o</u>'s in <u>tooth</u> and <u>foot</u> the same or different?

_____

_____

10 Are the <u>a</u>'s in <u>father</u> and <u>happy</u> the same or different?

_____

_____

11 Are the <u>e</u>'s in <u>ear</u> and <u>clear</u> the same or different?

_____

_____

12 Are the <u>u</u>'s in <u>mountain</u> and <u>mouth</u> the same or different?

_____

_____

1 This is _____a_____ hand.   These are _hands_.

2 This is _____an_____ arm.   These are _____.

3 This is _____ woman.   These are _____.

4 This is _____ eye.   These are _____.

5 This is _____ potato.   These are _____.

6 This is _____ orange.   These are _____.

7 This is _____ foot.   These are _____.

8 This is _____ baby.   These are _____.

9 This is _____ shelf.   These are _____.

10 This is _____ shoe.   These are _____.

11 This is _____ toe.

These are _____.

12 This is _____ inch.

These are _____.

13 This is _____ knife.

These are _____.

14 This is _____ leaf.

These are _____.

15 This is _____ body.

These are _____.

16 This is _____ tooth. These are _____.

17 This is _____ stocking. These are _____.

18 This is _____ thumb. These are _____.

19 This is _____ flower. These are _____.

20 This is _____ question mark.

These are _____ _____.

She (<u>is putting</u>, putting, will putting) water in a pot.

1 He (go, will going, goes) to the store with his father.

2 She (make, is make, made) the baby happy when she gave his bottle to him.

3 They (was taking, took, were take) their hats off when they came in.

4 The man said, "(Put, Puts, Putting) the money in the box."

5 He (comes, came, is coming) to our house before he saw the Smith family.

6 The icebox (having, have, has) different sorts of things in it.

7 I (giving, am giving, gives) food to the animals.

8 The men (are doing, are do, does) what I said.

9 He (get, got, is got) his new coat at the clothing store.

10 She (say, are saying, says), "The meat is ready now, but the potatoes are not."

1 It is (air, water) which keeps an airplane up.

2 (Air, Ice) is solid but (ice, water) is a liquid.

3 (Air, Ice) is not solid and it is not a liquid.

4 The (air, water) that we take in and give out is our breath.

5 When our breath comes out after going in, it is (cold, warm).

6 The air in the icebox is (warm, cold).

7 The (heat, light) of a flame will make the air over it warm.

8 The water in a pot over a flame is (warm, cold).

9 An (airplane, animal) goes through the air.

10 Steam is (a liquid, not a liquid) and it is (solid, not solid).

1 <u>He and she</u> are coming out of the store.

   _They_____ are coming out of the store.

2 <u>He and I</u> will go to the house together.

   _____ will go to the house together.

3 <u>You and she</u> have new hats.

   _____ have new hats.

4 <u>Mr. and Ms. Smith</u> have two sons and one daughter.

   _____ have two sons and one daughter.

5 <u>You and I</u> are persons.

   _____ are persons.

6 She will get some bread and cheese for <u>you and me</u>.
   She will get some bread and cheese

   for _____.

7 Mr. Smith will give a dog to his <u>son and daughter</u>.
   Mr. Smith will give a dog to _____.

8 <u>They and I</u> will come to see you.

_____ will come to see you.

9 The man gave some apples to <u>her and him</u>.

The man gave some apples to _____.

10 <u>You and he</u> have milk in your glasses. _____

have milk in your glasses.

11 A box is on <u>the table</u>.

A box is on _____.

12 He took <u>his hat and coat</u> off the hook.

He took _____ off the hook.

13 The baby was with <u>Mr. Smith</u>.

The baby was with _____.

14 The airplane was over <u>the trees</u>.

The airplane was over _____.

15 <u>The woman</u> gave <u>the gloves</u> to <u>Ms. Smith</u>.

_____ gave _____

to _____.

1 A _foot_ is twelve inches.

2 A yard is _____ feet.

3 A tree is one sort of _____.

4 An icebox is a box for keeping food

   _____.

5 Dresses are clothing for _____.

6 A breadbox is a _____ in which we
   keep bread.

7 A girl is her mother's and father's _____.

8 A room is a _____ of a house.

9 A baby is a _____ or a daughter of a
   man and woman.

10 Breath is _____ which we take in
   through the nose and mouth.

11 Soup is a liquid _____.

12 A clock is an _____ for measuring time.

13 Cheese is a sort _____ food which we make from milk.

14 _____ are clothing for the hands.

15 The _____ are the part of the body for seeing.

16 The part of a person's face which is under his mouth is his _____.

17 The _____ is the front of the head.

18 The pages of a book are the part between its _____.

19 The mouth is for taking _____ and drink and for saying things.

20 A _____ is a part of a chest or table in which we put things.

<u>are</u>   <u>did</u>   <u>does</u>   <u>do</u>   <u>is</u>   <u>makes</u>   <u>make</u>
<u>making</u>   <u>was</u>   <u>were</u>

1 The dog <u>does</u> not get a bone before
  Mrs. Hubbard goes out.

2 The boys _____ coming to this house,
  aren't they?

3 We _____ not keep apples in an icebox.

4 She _____ not see Tommy when she
  went to the store.

5 He _____ not making shelves for his
  books now.

6 We do not _____ clear soup with milk.

7 Three of the men _____ putting boxes
  on shelves when he went in.

8 Ms. Smith _____ all Mary's dresses.

9 The man _____ not going to his house
  but Johnny said he was.

10 The heat is _____ the butter soft.

1 Question: _When did she put it_
in the basket?

   Answer: She put it in the basket after she took it
   from the tree.

2 Question: _____

   _____

   Answer: My dog is the dog with long legs and a
   short tail.

3 Question: _____

   _____

   Answer: The liquid which is in the glass is water.

4 Question: _____

   _____

   Answer: The man at the window is Mr. Smith.

5 Question: _____

   _____

   Answer: My nose is between my eyes and my
   mouth.

6 Question: _____

_____

Answer: I got my new coat yesterday.

7 Question: _____

_____

Answer: The girl who has long hair is Mary Smith.

8 Question: _____

_____

Answer: The key is in my pocket.

9 Question: _____

_____

Answer: The thing which I have in my hand is a
fork.

10 Question: _____

_____

Answer: Mary is making soup.

who   which   what

1 Do you see _who_ is in the glass?

2 That is _____ I said to them.

3 I have the book _____ you gave to me.

4 This is the boy _____ has the orange.

5 He is the man _____ was on the ship with me.

6 She did not say _____ of these keys was in the drawer.

7 I will see _____ is in the box.

8 _____ he sees he takes.

9 Where is the girl _____ got the new dress?

10 She gave him an apple _____ he put in his pocket.

1 _What_ did you say to him?

2 _____ is Tom Green's house?

3 _____ is the time?

4 _____ of these two apples will you take?

5 _____ will go to the store with me?

6 _____ put it there?

7 _____ hat is yours?

8 _____ do you see on the floor?

9 _____ took the book from the shelf?

10 _____ is that thing on the table?

1 The girl's (herfat) __father__ and mother are coming into the room.

2 Oranges are one (tros) _____ of fruit.

3 The (etha) _____ of the flame is making the water warm.

4 He is having a (knird) _____ of water.

5 That is the Smiths' (shueo) _____.

6 A flame gives off heat and (thilg) _____.

7 The book is on the (felsh) _____.

8 Soup is a (quidli) _____.

9 Plants come up out of the (thare) _____.

10 Milk is not a (racel) _____ liquid.

11 Some mountains are (gihh) _____.

12 When water is (nilgibo) _____ it gives off steam.

13 Fruit trees put out flowers (bofeer) _____ they put out fruit.

14 Do you keep knives and forks in a (dwerar) _____?

15 THe put down one spoon and took up (hotrane) _____.

16 Cows (vieg) _____ milk and meat to us.

17 Her coat was on a (okho) _____.

18 The girl gave a (husp) _____ to the drawer.

19 He will take the skin off the apple with a (nekfi) _____.

20 Do you put (tutreb) on bread?

1 THIS BOTTLE TOOK WHICH MARY FROM IS THE MILK THIS.

This is the milk which Mary took from this bottle.

2 NOT THE THE ON GIRL FLOOR SEE MONEY THE DOES.

_____

_____

3 ON BETWEEN THE THE I A WINDOW THE WILL AND WALL PICTURE PUT DOOR.

_____

_____

4 NOT IS SHUT DOOR THE.

_____

_____

5 FOR AN TIME CLOCK A MEASURING IS INSTRUMENT.

_____

_____

6 WHICH THE YOU IS GAVE CHEESE WHERE I TO?

_____

_____

7 AFTER IN THE BASKET THE TOOK APPLE SHE OFF
SHE THE PUT TABLE IT.

_____

_____

8 FOOT ARE THICK THE HOUSE OF A WALLS THE.

_____

_____

9 AN THING MY HAVE ORANGE IN WHICH THE I
IS HAND.

_____

_____

10 AIR ICEBOX THE KEEPS COLD FOOD THE COLD
IN THE.

_____

_____

<u>off</u>   <u>up</u>   <u>of</u>   <u>with</u>   <u>under</u>
<u>on</u>   <u>in</u>   <u>for</u>   <u>before</u>   <u>through</u>

A 1 The airplane went _____up_____ into the air.

  2 There are two dogs _____ the room.

  3 Men and women and boys and girls are different
   sorts _____ persons.

  4 Ms. Smith will put the plates of soup
   _____ the table.

  5 She took the skin _____ the orange
   with a knife.

  6 My mouth is _____ my nose.

  7 The number six comes _____ the
   number seven.

  8 A clock is an instrument _____
   measuring time.

  9 I will go into the other room _____
   that door.

  10 Tom is at the window _____ his mother.

between   at   down   after   to
with   into   over   from   out of

B 1 Three is ___between___ two and four.

2 The key went out of his hand and down
_____ the water.

3 The apple is on the branch _____ your
head.

4 Ms. Smith gave a glass of water _____
her son.

5 We get milk _____ cows.

6 The number nine is _____ the number
eight.

7 When Mr. Smith came into the room Mr. Jones
went _____ it.

8 She is taking the skin off the potato
_____ a knife.

9 The birds came _____ from the tree for
some bits of bread.

10 The boy and girl are in their seats
_____ the table.

C 1 The baby is (in, <u>on</u>) the floor.

2 She sees the steam coming (out of, for) the pot.

3 He put his hat and coat (on, from).

4 Mary is crushing the potatoes (by, with) a fork.

5 This is a plate (for, of) soup but there is no soup in it.

6 They will be here (on, in) a short time.

7 You were going to the store (to, for) some new shoes.

8 An airplane goes (through, over) the air.

9 There are different things (into, on) the shelf.

10 We make butter (from, off) milk.

When John Smith came to the door of his house, he put his hand in his coat pocket. There was a knife in his pocket, but there was no key.

"Where is my key?" he said. "It is not in my pocket. It was in this pocket. Now there is a knife in this pocket, but there is no key." He put his hand in the other pockets of his coat, but there was no key in them.

"Mary has a key," he said, "but Mary is not here. She will be here at 5:00. Now it is 3:00. From 3:00 to 5:00 is a long time."

Mr. Smith went from the door of his house to the front window. The window was shut. He went to one side of the house and to the back of the house and to the other side of the house. All the windows were shut. Then he came to the front of the house again.

"I will take my open knife and see what it will do," he said. He went to the front window and put the thin part of his knife under it. The window went up an inch. Then he put his fingers under the window and gave a push.

Now the window was open. Mr. Smith put one leg and then the other through the open window.

"Now I am in the house," he said.

He was out of breath. He went to a seat. There was a man's coat over the back of the seat. "Here is my other coat," said Mr. Smith. "Is my key in one of the pockets of this coat? I will see."

The coat had four pockets. Mr. Smith put his hand in three of the pockets. No key! When he put his hand in the other pocket, there it was. Mr. Smith took the key out of the pocket and said, "Now I have my key. It was there all the time!"

1 What was in the pocket of the coat which John Smith had on?

There was a knife in the pocket of the
coat which John Smith had on.

2 Who had a key to the door?

_____

_____

3 What time was it when John Smith came to the door of his house?

_____

_____

4 Did Mary come back before John got in?

_____

_____

5 Were the windows of the house open or shut?

_____

_____

6 Did John get one window an inch open with his fingers or with a knife?

_____

_____

7 What did John see over the back of a seat in his house?

_____

_____

8 Where was John's key?

_____

_____

9 Did John get his key before he got into his house?

_____

_____

10 Through which window did John get into his house?

_____

_____

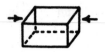

These are two sides of the <u>same</u> box.
The sides are the <u>same</u>. They are not
<u>different</u> from one another.

1 These are two sides of the _____ thing.
The two sides are _____ from one another.

2 These are two windows of the _____ house.
They are the _____. They are not
_____ from one another.

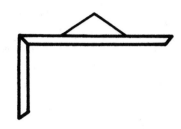

3 These are two _____ of the same picture
  frame. One side is _____ from the other.
  The two sides are not the _____.

4 These are two covers of a _____. They are
  from the _____ book, but they
  are _____ from one another. The front
  cover of the book is _____ from the back.

What are these men and boys doing? The two men are on their knees doing something to a boy who is face down. One of these men took the boy from the water after seeing him go under. The man went in after him with all his clothing on.

Now they are turning the boy over. "See, his eyes are shut," some of the other boys say.

"Keep back, will you," says the man who went into the water, putting out an arm and pushing them back.

"He has to have air."

"We've got all the water out of him," says the other man, "but he isn't breathing, or is he?"

He puts his ear to the boy's chest. "No," he says. "He isn't breathing."

Now one man is opening the boy's mouth and the other is putting his mouth to the boy's mouth. He is breathing air into the boy. He is making his breath go in and out of the boy. He does this again and again.

"Give me a glass, someone," he is saying now.

A man is taking his glasses off his nose and handing them to him.

"Good! These will do," he says, taking them and putting one glass in front of the boy's mouth.

"Is he breathing?" says the man who took the boy from the water. "Yes, he is. See!"

They see the boy's breath on the glass. He is breathing again. He is going to be all right. The air is going in and out of his chest.

They got him out of the water in time.

1 Which boy in the picture was in the water?

The boy who is face down in the picture was in the water.

2 Where was this boy before the two men put him down on his face?

3 What do they put in front of the boy's mouth to see if he is breathing?

4 Does one of the men give some of his breath to the boy?

5 What makes the men say that the boy is breathing?

6 Is our breath a part of us?

ANSWERS

The first number indicates the page of the workbook on which the questions appear. The number in parentheses refers to the pages in *English Re-start, Book 1* which these exercises support.

Pages 128-129 (4-7)

1 She is here.
2 It is there.
3 They are here.
4 They are there.

5 You are here.
6 They are here.
7 You are there.
8 We are here.

Pages 130-131 (8-10)

A 1 table
2 hand
3 thumb
4 fingers

B 1 man, is
2 there, She

Pages 132-133 (11-13)

1 (<u>his</u>, her, my)
2 (left, <u>right</u>, the)
3 (<u>Her</u>, His, Its)

4 (<u>in</u>, my, on)
5 (finger, <u>head</u>, thumb)
6 (in, here, <u>on</u>)

Pages 134-135 (14-16)

1 taking, was
2 put, is

3 will put, is
4 took, is

Pages 136-137 (17-18)

A 1 hands

2 men

3 These

4 women

B 1 man's, his

2 woman's, her

3 are

4 women's

Pages 138-139 (19-22)

4	She is putting her hat on.
2	These are bottles.
1	He gave his hat to her.
3	The ship is on the water.
6	He will put the bottle on the table.
8	She is taking it off the table.
5	He is putting the hat on the table.
7	He will give the bottle to him.

Page 140 (23-25)

1 in

2 on

3 These

4 It

5 there

6 here

7 Those

8 They

9 These

10 its

11 an, a

12 feet

Page 141 (26-27)

1 Two windows are in a wall .

2 They are shut.

3 The door of the room is open.

236

4 A picture is on a wall.
5 It is a picture of a ship.
6 The ship is on the water.
7 The picture is in a frame.
8 It is on a cord.
9 The cord is on a hook.
10 The hook is in a wall.

Pages 142-143 (28-29)

1 street, will
2 is, going
3 went, is, was
4 at, of, shut, open

Page 144 (30)

1 Is this a house?
4 What is that?
5 Is this a table?
7 What are these?
10 What is this?
14 Is that a picture?
16 What is a question?

Page 145 (27-30)

1 It is a frame.
2 No, it is not a hook. It is a cord.
3 Yes, it is a picture of a man and woman.

Pages 146-147 (35-36)

1 three, two, four
2 four, three, five
3 seven, six, eight
4 ten
5 five
6 eight

A 1 man, person
2 clock, thing
3 woman, person
4 house, thing

B 1 Yes, she is a person.
2 No, he is not a thing.
He is a person.

1 (are, <u>are not</u>)
2 (<u>is</u>, is not)
3 (is, <u>is not</u>)
(are, <u>are not</u>)

4 (<u>are</u>, are not)
5 (are, <u>are not</u>)
6 (<u>was</u>, was not)
(<u>was</u>, was not)

A 1 I am saying "nose."
2 She does not see me.
3 She sees.
4 He did not see.
5 It is not open.

B 1 eyes, shut
2 His, are
3 One, is
4 Her, open
5 He, saying
6 She, bottle

A 1 on, over
2 on, under
3 between

4 of, on
5 of, at

B 1 A seat is under the clock.
2 A glass is on the table.
3 No, they are not on the seat.
They are on the floor.

  4 Five and six are between four and seven on the clock.

  5 They are a glass, a bottle and a book.

Pages 156-157 (45-46)

  1 The short hand is between nine and ten.

  2 The long hand is at six.

  3 or 4. The short hand is at four.

  4 or 3. There is no long hand.

  5 or 6. Her ears are under her hair.

  6 or 5. Her hand is over a part of her face.

  7 or 8. It has a face.

  8 or 7. It has no eyes or ears.

Page 158 (46)

1 before	5 between	9 before
2 before	6 Ten	10 after
3 after	7 Seven	11 between
4 after	8 Eight, nine	12 part

Page 159 (47)

Do, other, them, Then, again

Pages 160-161 (48-49)

A 1 The seat's feet are number 6.

  2 The baby's feet are number 2.

  3 The dog's feet are number 1.

  4 The man's hands are number 3.

  5 The clock's hands are number 4.

B 1 eyes
  2 nose
  3 mouth
  4 parts
  5 head

  6 tail
  7 body
  8 dog's legs
  9 parts
 10 house

Pages 162-163 (50-51)

1 Yes, it is a part of a leg.
2 No, it is not.
  or It is a part of a foot.
3 No, our necks are not parts of our faces.
4 My chin is under my mouth.
5 Yes, a chest of drawers is a thing.
6 Yes, a chest is a part of a body.
7 Yes, my eyes are parts of my face.
8 No, my nose is under my eyes.
9 Yes, my ears are parts of my head.
10 The part of a man which is between his head, his arms and his legs is his body.

Pages 164-165 (58-61)

1 The man's name is Jim Wilson.
2 He is putting his hand in his pocket.
3 He will take his door key from his pocket.
4 He will put his key in the lock of the door.
5 He will give a push to the door.
6 The door is shut now.
7 Ms. Wilson will come to the door.
8 Mr. Wilson will take his hat off.
9 Yes, he will take Ms. Wilson's hand in his.
10 They will go into the house together.

Page 166 (60-63)

1 one, other
2 another, others
3 other
4 one, other
5 One, others

6 another
7 One, others
8 One, other
9 one, another
10 one, another

Page 167 (60-63)

A 1 at
2 into
3 in
4 out of
5 to

B 1 is coming
2 came
3 will go
4 are going
5 went

Page 169 (64-69)

1 He put his hat on the table before he went out.
2 No, it isn't on the table.
3 She put his hat in another room.
4 Yes, she came into the room at four.
5 He went out of the room at three.

Page 170 (70-73)

1 (take, <u>took</u>, taking)
2 (seeing, saw, <u>see</u>)
3 (gave, <u>give</u>, giving)
4 (taking, took, <u>take</u>)
5 (go, <u>going</u>, went)
6 (putting, puts, <u>put</u>)

7 (<u>come</u>, coming, came)
8 (going, went, <u>go</u>)
9 (<u>says</u>, say, saying)
10 (seeing, see, <u>sees</u>)
11 (<u>when</u>, again, did)
12 (<u>Did</u>, What, Where)

Page 171 (74-76)

1	Was	6	Does
2	What	7	Will
3	Is	8	Who
4	When	9	Where
5	Did	10	Are

Page 173 (77-78)

1 She was getting the soup when he came in.
2 Yes, it was Tom who put his hat on a hook on the door.
3 There were two plates of soup in Alice's hands.
4 Tom put the glasses of water on the table.
5 No, Alice took her seat at the table before Tom.

Pages 174-175 (79-81)

A 1 from a clothing store
   2 in his mouth
   3 in her hand
   4 on his feet
   5 of a leg

B 1 at a store
   2 with a spoon
   3 on her hands
   4 over the store
   5 under the table

Page 176 (80-81)

1	gloves	5	hats
2	shoes	6	stockings
3	new	7	shoes
4	clothing store	8	old

A 1 (after, <u>before</u>)   2 (<u>after</u>, before)
B 1 (<u>after</u>, before)   2 (after, <u>before</u>)
C 1 (<u>which</u>, when)   2 (which, <u>when</u>)

Page 179 (84-85)

1 What   4 left, coat, arm   7 take, door, key
2 name   5 street, box   8 baby, box
3 putting   6 cover, front

Pages 180-181 (86-91)

out, hands, were, tray, put, took, on,
an, of, on, is, potato, soup, and, said,
on, the other, What, get, We, gets, Then,
bottles, finger, Is, No, that, is, animals,
took, some, gave, she, do, get, from, milk

Pages 182-183 (92-93)

1 Will the woman put the cover on the pot?
2 Was the water in the pot boiling?
3 Is an apple a fruit?
4 Did she take the skin off the potato?
5 Do the roots of a plant go down into the earth?
6 Were there flowers on the plants?
7 Are these leaves of a plant?
8 When water is boiling does it give off steam?
9 Is there a flame under the pot?
10 Has a flower a stem?

A 1 Water is turned into ice when we make it cold in a tray.

2 The heat of the flame makes water in a pot over a flame give off steam.

3 No, steam is not solid.

4 Yes, ice is solid.

5 No, water is a liquid.

B 1 No, air is not solid.

2 No, air is not a liquid.

3 No, we do not see air.

4 Air which we take in and give out through our noses and mouths is our breath.

5 Yes, the air which we give out is warm air.

C 1 The girl in the picture is at a window in an airplane.

2 Yes, the plane is up in the air.

3 No, the air up there is cold.

4 She sees other airplanes through the window of the plane.

5 No, birds do not go 10,000 feet up in the air.

D 1 In the picture the girl is at a window.

2 Yes, the glass of the window is cold.

3 Yes, the girl's breath is turning to water on the cold glass of the window.

4 Yes, there is steam on the glass of the window in front of the girl's mouth.

5 She is making a mark on it with her finger.

Page 188 (96-97)

1 (<u>instrument</u>, inch)

2 (<u>yard</u>, foot)

3 (feet, <u>inches</u>)

4 (<u>eggs</u>, milk)

5 (<u>for</u>, of)
6 (<u>keeps</u>, takes)
7 (<u>measure</u>, measuring)

8 (<u>Measuring</u>, Getting)
9 (<u>long</u>, short)
10 (<u>very</u>, not)

Page 189 (98-101)

1 (<u>meat</u>, books)
2 (<u>bread</u>, oranges)
3 (<u>cheese</u>, potatoes)
4 (<u>oranges</u>, bread)
5 (<u>drink</u>, glass)
6 (<u>good</u>, bad)
7 (thin, <u>thick</u>)
8 (happy, <u>not happy</u>)

9 (<u>butter</u>, an egg)
10 (<u>thin</u>, thick)
11 (<u>happy</u>, not happy)
12 (<u>hard</u>, soft)
13 (good, <u>bad</u>)
14 (<u>five-thirty</u>, five-forty)
15 (<u>soft</u>, hard)

Pages 190-191 (100-105)

1 No, eggs in an egg box are not ready for the table.
2 Yes, it is.
3 No, some flames are high.
4 No, some buildings are low.
5 It is a fruit.
6 Yes, it does.
7 We see that they are soft when a fork will go through them.
8 Yes, it is.
9 Yes, we do.
10 The thick walls keep the heat from the things in an icebox.

Pages 192-193 (102-105)

1 One of these buildings is high but the other is not.

2 The boy has a bit of cheese between his teeth.
3 Ms. Jones is crushing the potatoes with a fork.
4 The woman is tasting the soup.
5 Glass is hard but butter is soft.
6 Mary is taking an orange off the plate.

Page 194 (106-107)

1 different sorts
2 the same, different
3 sort
4 different
5 the same
6 different
7 food

Page 195 (108-112)

1 Which, butter, which
2 Which, apple, which
3 Which, book, which
4 Which, pipe, which
5 Which, hat, which
6 Which, house, which

Pages 196-197 (108-109)

1 boys, girl
2 family
3 father
4 mother
5 daughter
6 sons
7 family
8 brothers
9 sister
10 father, mother

Pages 198-199 (110-112)

1 That is the man who was on the mountain.
2 This is the cheese which was in the icebox.
3 This is Ms. Jones who put the cheese in the icebox.
4 This is the milk which John got.

5 This is the potato soup which Mary made.
6 That is the water which is clear.
7 This is the bone which was in the dog's mouth.
8 This is the spoon which was in Tom's hand.
9 This is Jane who came to our house.
10 This is the dog who had a bone in his mouth.

Pages 200-201 (108-112)

1 Yes, the <u>i</u> is the same.
2 The <u>o</u>'s are different.
3 The <u>a</u>'s are different.
4 The <u>o</u>'s are the same.
5 The <u>a</u>'s are different.
6 The <u>i</u>'s are the same.
7 The <u>a</u>'s are the same.
8 The <u>u</u>'s are the same.
9 The <u>o</u>'s are different. (The <u>o</u>'s in <u>tooth</u> are like the <u>o</u>'s in <u>room</u>. The <u>o</u>'s in <u>foot</u> are like the <u>o</u>'s in <u>good</u>.)
10 The <u>a</u>'s are different.
11 The <u>e</u>'s are the same.
12 The <u>u</u>'s are the same.

Pages 202-205 (1-112)

1 a, hands
2 an, arms
3 a, women
4 an, eyes
5 a, potatoes
6 an, oranges
7 a, feet
8 a, babies
9 a, shelves
10 a, shoes
11 a, toes
12 an, inches
13 a, knives
14 a, leaves

15	a, bodies	18	a, thumbs
16	a, teeth	19	a, flowers
17	a, stockings	20	a, question marks

Page 206 (1-112)

1 (go, will going, <u>goes</u>)
2 (make, is make, <u>made</u>)
3 (was taking, <u>took</u>, were take)
4 (<u>Put</u>, Puts, Putting)
5 (comes, <u>came</u>, is coming)

6 (having, have, <u>has</u>)
7 (giving, <u>am giving</u>, gives)
8 (<u>are doing</u>, are do, does)
9 (get, <u>got</u>, is got)
10 (say, are saying, <u>says</u>)

Page 207 (1-112)

1 (<u>air</u>, water)
2 (Air, <u>Ice</u>) (ice, <u>water</u>)
3 (<u>Air</u>, Ice)
4 (<u>air</u>, water)
5 (cold, <u>warm</u>)

6 (warm, <u>cold</u>)
7 (<u>heat</u>, light)
8 (<u>warm</u>, cold)
9 (<u>airplane</u>, animal)
10 (a liquid, <u>not a liquid</u>) (solid, <u>not solid</u>)

Pages 208-209 (1-112)

1	They	6	us	11	it
2	We	7	them	12	them
3	You	8	We	13	him
4	They	9	them	14	them
5	We	10	You	15	She, them, her

1 foot	8 part	15 eyes
2 three	9 Son	16 chin
3 plant	10 air	17 face
4 cold	11 food	18 covers
5 women or girls	12 instrument	19 food
6 box	13 of	20 drawer
7 daughter	14 Gloves	

1 does	5 is	9 was
2 are	6 make	10 making
3 do	7 were	
4 did	8 makes	

1 When did she put it in the basket?
2 Which is your dog?
3 What is this liquid in the glass?
4 Who is that man at the window?
5 Where is your nose?
6 When did you get your new coat?
7 Who is that girl with long hair?
8 Where is the key?
9 What is this thing in your hand?
10 What is Mary doing?

1 what	5 who	9 who
2 what	6 which	10 which
3 which	7 what	
4 who	8 What	

1 What	5 Who	9 Who
2 Which	6 Who	10 What
3 What	7 Which	
4 Which	8 What	

1 father	8 liquid	15 another
2 sort	9 earth	16 give
3 heat	10 clear	17 hook
4 drink	11 high	18 push
5 house	12 boiling	19 knife
6 light	13 before	20 butter
7 shelf	14 drawer	

1 This is the milk which Mary took from this bottle.
2 The girl does not see the money on the floor.
3 I will put a picture on the wall between the door and the window. *Or*, I will put a picture on the wall between the window and the door.
4 The door is not shut.
5 A clock is an instrument for measuring time.

6 Where is the cheese which I gave to you?
7 After she took the apple off the table, she put it in the basket. *Or,* She put the apple in the basket after she took it off the table.
8 The walls of the house are a foot thick.
9 The thing which I have in my hand is an orange.
10 The cold air in the icebox keeps the food cold.

Pages 221-223 (1-112)

A 1 up
2 in
3 of
4 on
5 off
6 under
7 before
8 for
9 through
10 with

B 1 between
2 into
3 over
4 to
5 from
6 after
7 out of
8 with
9 down
10 at

C 1 (in, <u>on</u>)
2 (<u>out of</u>, for)
3 (<u>on</u>, from)
4 (by, <u>with</u>)
5 (<u>for</u>, of)
6 (on, <u>in</u>)
7 (to, <u>for</u>)
8 (<u>through</u>, over)
9 (into, <u>on</u>)
10 (<u>from</u>, off)

Pages 226-227 (1-112)

1 There was a knife in the pocket of the coat which John Smith had on.
2 Mary had a key to the door.

3 It was 3:00 when John Smith came to the door of his house.
4 No, Mary didn't come back before John got in.
5 The windows of the house were shut.
6 John got the window an inch open with his knife.
7 John saw his other coat over the back of the seat.
8 John's key was in one of the pockets of his other coat in the house.
9 No, John didn't get his key before he got into his house.
10 John got into the house through the front window of his house.

Pages 228-229 (1-112)

1 same, different
2 same, same, different
3 sides, different, same
4 book, same, different, different

Page 232 (1-112)

1 The boy who is face down in the picture was in the water.
2 The boy was in the water before the two men put him down on his face.
3 They put one glass in front of the boy's mouth to see if he is breathing.
4 Yes, one of the men gives some of his breath to the boy.
5 They see the boy's breath on the glass.
6 Yes, our breath is a part of us.

INDEX

English Re-start Basic

초판 1쇄 발행 2008년 7월 7일
      120쇄 발행 2009년 11월 30일

지은이 I. A. Richards, Christine Gibson.
발행인 최봉수
총편집인 이수미
편집인 양은숙
에디터 김경진

디자인 구수연
전산편집 조영라
마케팅 박성인, 김현오, 이상호, 임현석
제작 한동수, 류정옥

임프린트 **NEWRUN**
주소 서울시 종로구 동숭동 199-16 웅진빌딩 5층
주문전화 02-3670-1570,1571 팩스 02-747-1239
문의전화 02-3670-1150 이메일 best79@wjbooks.co.kr

발행처 (주)웅진씽크빅
출판신고 1980년 3월 29일 제 406-2007-00046호

한국어판 출판권 ⓒ (주)웅진씽크빅 2008
ISBN 978-89-01-08335-3 14740
     978-89-01-08334-6 (세트)

The number after each word indicates the page of the text on which the word first occurs.

A a 8
after 30
again 39
air 95
airplane 95
all 49
am 4
an 25
and 23
animal 91
another 61
answer 30
apple 82
are 5
arm 25
at 29

B baby 49
back 84
bad 98
basket 82
be 35
before 46
between 43
bird 24
bit 103
body 49
boiling 93
bone 112

book 38
bookshelves 44
bottle 22
box 84
boy 37
branch 82
bread 99
breadbox 99
breath 95
brother 109
building 104
but 38
butter 99

C came 61
cheese 99
chest 51
chin 50
clear 110
clock 35
clothing 81
coat 84
cold 94
come 60
cord 27
cover 43
cow 91
crushing 102
cup 91

D daughter 108
did 41
different 106
do 47
does 41
dog 44
doing 77
dollar 74
door 26
down 76
drawer 51
dress 80
drink 98

E ear 45
earth 92
egg 96
eight 36
eleven 36
eye 40

F face 45
family 109
father 108
feet 25
fifty 101
finger 10
five 35
flame 93
floor 23